I Rest My Case . . .

I Rest
My Case . . .

Unpublished Letters to
The Daily Telegraph

EDITED BY
IAIN HOLLINGSHEAD

First published 2011 by
Aurum Press Limited
7 Greenland Street
London NW1 0ND
www.aurumpress.co.uk

A catalogue record for this book
is available from the British Library.

ISBN 978 1 84513 690 1
Ebook ISBN 978 1 84513 740 3

10 9 8 7 6 5 4 3 2
2015 2014 2013 2012 2011

Typeset by MRules

Printed in Great Britain by Clays Ltd, St Ives plc

CONTENTS

SIR – I hope your letter page authors haven't enjoyed as much as I have browsing through ... ... should they have found one in their character, it is a feast of humour and I am flattered ... ... personal entries. Is it too to ... ... complete a trilogy?

David Harridge
Unby, Leicestershire

SIR – I know why I so enjoy ... ... to the future. The world is falling down around us ... ... today, apart from the serious ... ... that mentions Beatrix Potter, ... are a pleasure to read.

Only your readers could turn ... ... turmoil to discuss recipes for ... ... to have your wedding reception ... ... episode of The Archers and who ... ... mother on Mothering Sunday.

On a personal note, the other ... ... an avid fan of this column is that ... ... I am the only one to have had a photograph ... ... in a swimsuit and on a Saturday.

Rosemary Almond
Hoddesdon, Hertfordshire

SIR — I hope your letter-page addicts have enjoyed as much as I have browsing through *I Could Go On*, should they have found one in their stocking. It is a feast of humour and I am flattered to have found two personal entries. Is it too much to hope that Iain will complete a trilogy?

David Hartridge
Groby, Leicestershire

SIR — I know why I so enjoy Letters to the Editor. The world is falling down around our ears and yet today, apart from the serious bit at the top (and even that mentions Beatrix Potter), the rest of the letters are a pleasure to read.

Only your readers could find time amidst the turmoil to discuss: recipes for Bloody Marys, when to have your wedding reception so as not to miss an episode of *The Archers* and what not to buy your mother on Mothering Sunday.

On a personal note, the other reason I am such an avid fan of this column is that, among my friends, I am the only one to have had a photograph printed, in a swimsuit and on a Saturday.

Rosemary Almond
Hoddesdon, Hertfordshire

SIR – In the past Britons travelled in perilous and near-impossible conditions to carve out an Empire; now they are reduced to using the letters pages of *The Daily Telegraph* to swap ideas on the best way to carry keys. As with everything else, I blame New Labour.

Keith Haines
Belfast

INTRODUCTION

Last Christmas, when we published *I Could Go On . . .*, we hoped our readers would pick up the hint in the title. True to form, the letters have continued to pour in, tackling everything from defence cuts to looters, from Rupert Murdoch to the tell-tell signs that your wife is turning into your mother-in-law.

What has been a bad year for some parts of the media has been an especially good one for our wonderful letter-writers. Even in this digital age our postbag continues to groan under the weight of correspondence. Our email inbox is crammed to overflowing. Our fax machine, perhaps the busiest in London (perhaps the *only* one in London), whirrs away contentedly. We've never felt the need to hack into our readers' phones to find out what they're thinking.

All these surplus thoughts, however whimsical, hilariously off-message or downright rude, have made the task of collating a third volume of unpublished letters more enjoyable than ever. Who would have thought a year ago that letter writers would be able to draw parallels between Silvio Berlusconi and the Duke of York, Andrew Marr and Ryan Giggs, or even the Archbishop of Canterbury and Rebekah Brooks (you'll have to turn to Chapter Five for that one)?

This has been the year of riots, Nick Clegg's

tears, bunga bunga, superinjunctions and the Blairs' bedroom revelations (again). England turned out to be surprisingly good at cricket and unsurprisingly bad at football world cup bids. The eurozone threatened to collapse altogether, as did half the Middle East. We waved goodbye to bin Laden, and an enthusiastic hello to Pippa Middleton's bottom.

Big events often bring out the best in our letter-writers. So, too, does the quotidian, whether a routine visit to the shops, catching a train or simply turning on the television. Perhaps *I Rest My Case* feels like more of a review of the year than our first two collections, but it also provides a further glimpse into the preoccupations of the mythical everyman, his frustrations and peccadilloes, hobbyhorses and fears. One of the most satisfying parts of editing such a compilation is when one letter, sent with faint hope of recognition into the void, finds an echo, however muffled, in another, and a form of conversation ensues between two or more complete strangers.

At the risk of sounding as unhinged as M, our regular correspondent from Bristol, who believes himself to be the head of MI6, I feel, after a couple of fond years in our letter-writers' irrepressible company, that I know them rather well. To all our correspondents, published, unpublished and now unpublished published, my grateful thanks — as well as to Christopher Howse, the letters editor; Matt Pritchett; Caroline Buckland; Richard Preston and everyone at Aurum. A particular thank you must also go to Sally Peck, the acting deputy letters editor, who did a huge amount of invaluable work sifting through the letters as they came in and applying her expert eye to separate the wheat from the chaff.

For now we rest our case, but am I alone in hoping we'll see you all again next year?

Iain Hollingshead
The Daily Telegraph
August 2011

KINGS, QUEENS AND JOKERS

THE PEOPLE'S PRIME MINISTER

SIR — This morning at breakfast, my mother opined that the real reason the Blairs haven't been invited to the Royal Wedding is that Cherie Blair might forget where she is and start trying to have another baby.

Thus, she is saved from herself. (And so are we.)

Felicity J. Foulis Brown
Bramley, Hampshire

SIR — Perhaps like mine, Tony Blair's invitation got 'lost in the post'.

Piers Casimir-Mrowczynski
Gustard Wood, Hertfordshire

SIR — Could any reader put their hand on their heart and say that they would invite to their grandson's wedding the people who stole their yacht?

James Cox
Lower Hardres, Kent

SIR – It's an absolute disgrace that the Blairs did not receive invitations; we have been deprived of our right to bid for them on eBay.

D.D.J.B.
Wellesbourne, Warwickshire

KATE MIDDLETON UNDER THE MAGNIFYING GLASS

SIR – There were four photographs of Kate Middleton in the paper on Saturday. One thing puzzles me: how does she keep the hat on at that angle? I have used a magnifying glass and I am still puzzled.

Eddie Peart
Rotherham, South Yorkshire

SIR – Might we look forward to seeing a blank rectangular space in *The Daily Telegraph* with the caption underneath: 'Kate Middleton didn't go anywhere today'?

Bill Wade
Sheffield

SIR – Now that Kate Middleton has a coat of arms, can we expect that from April 29 the Middleton family will be known as the Uppertons?

Huw Beynon
Llandeilo, Carmarthenshire

SIR – Surely the Middleton coat of arms should have a cupcake and a party popper in it somewhere?

Mrs M.C. Kellett
Benenden, Kent

SIR – Do we have to be bored on an almost daily basis regarding this co-habiting, unemployed woman?

Primrose Peacock
Truro, Cornwall

SIR – Would it be possible to relax the law in Britain to allow Prince William to have five wives or more? Then we could have a Royal Wedding every year.

Gillian Lee
Norbury, Cheshire

SIR – Yawn, yawn, yawn. Promise me it will stop after the wedding.

Steve Cattell
Hougham, Lincolnshire

SIR – Given the day off school on May 6 1960, for the wedding of Antony Armstrong-Jones to Princess Margaret, I played cricket on the local recreation ground. I proudly scored my first and, so far, only century. There was one bowler, one fielder and one tennis ball.

I have already oiled my bat for April 29 this year.

Colin Henderson
Cranleigh, Surrey

FORGETTING SARAH FERGUSON

SIR – According to your article, the Duchess of York is making a documentary entitled 'Finding Sarah'. I wasn't aware that anyone was really bothering to search.

S.K.
Havant, Hampshire

SIR – For all her good charitable works why does Sarah, Duchess of York, at the age of 51, still feel the need to frequent nightclubs?

> **Doreen Edwards**
> Birchington, Kent

SIR – It's such a shame that the Duke and Duchess of York are divorced. They really are made for each other.

> **Peter Leatherbarrow**
> Wortwell, Norfolk

SIR – Would a more suitable role for the Duke of York be Trade Envoy to Italy? He and the Italian Prime Minister seem to have similar interests, and possibly, much in common.

> **Simon Butcher**
> West Mersea, Essex

SIR – I suggest that the Duke of York be replaced by Mr and Mrs Beckham.

> **Neville Shermer**
> Wooburn Common, Buckinghamshire

THE PEOPLE'S PRIME MINISTER II

SIR – If David Cameron is so anxious to appear at the Royal Wedding dressed as a man of the people, why doesn't he go the whole hog and wear a tracksuit and trainers?

John Franklin
London N1

SIR – Can the Foreign Secretary be persuaded to lend him his baseball cap?

Jeremy Burton
Radford, Oxfordshire

SIR – Does Mr Cameron know what happened to the man in Matthew 22: 11–14 who turned up to a wedding in inappropriate garments?

E.W.
Milton Keynes

SIR – If I were his valet, I would put out the correct dress and just tell him to put it on.

Lt. Col. John Arthur (retd.)
Ridgewell, Essex

SIR – Let us hope Mr Cameron does not remove his tie and jacket when he spots the cameras in the Abbey.

George Noon
Preston, Lancashire

SCOOPING THE ROYAL BARREL

SIR – While I very much enjoyed the Royal Wedding, I did miss the BBC failing to interview William and Kate on their way back down the aisle, asking, 'How does it feel?'

Bruce Ridge
Cleveden, Somerset

SIR – Yes, it was lovely, but what was all that vegetation doing in Westminster Abbey? It made the place look like it was harvest festival. I kept looking for one of those big loaves baked like a wheatsheaf and a few cans of peas and peaches.

John Alborough
Syleham, Suffolk

SIR – It is deeply shocking that *The Daily Telegraph*, of all newspapers, should refer to Prince William as 'the groom'. It should not be necessary to point out that Kate Middleton is not a horse.

Christopher Macy
Wellingore, Lincolnshire

SIR – I opened my *Telegraph* at nine o'clock on the morning of the Royal Wedding to read your description of the Queen's grandson's 'palpably happy marriage'. I know you like to be first with the news, but this is ridiculous.

Rev. Dr. Peter Mullen
London EC1

SIR – Today I was presented with 24 pages of articles, one editorial, a 'Brilliant Picture Supplement' and one cartoon. You, sir, are stark raving bonkers.

S.L.
Reading, Berkshire

SIR – Please, please, I implore you. No more photographs of that woman in that stupid hat. I cannot take any more. It is worse than being in Guantanamo Bay.

B. Lees
Manchester

SIR – Just watched the Royal Wedding on *Dave*. It was a very emotional ceremony. Good luck to Prince Charles and Diana in the future.

Stephen J.D. Wain
Cambridge

WHAT A LOVELY PIPPA!

SIR – While I was browsing the article by Judith Woods on the posterior of a certain bridesmaid, a young lady gracefully swayed past. A young man within earshot commented, 'What a lovely "Pippa" she has.' Has a new word entered our lexicon?

Ted Forsyth
Guildford, Surrey

SIR – Forget the wedding dress, let's display the lovely Pippa herself, preferably on the fourth plinth in Trafalgar Square.

Ronald Walford
South Darenth, Kent

SIR – In my humble opinion it seems totally appropriate that the girl with the shapeliest rear in the country should be on nothing less than the arm of a duke.

Joe Cobb
Nether Winchendon, Buckinghamshire

SIR – I have just noticed a striking resemblance between the photograph of Pippa Middleton and the 1656 painting 'Las Meninas' by Diego Velázquez. I don't suppose Pilates had been invented 355 years ago, but the young maid of honour still looks very slim and trim.

Siri Dennis
Farnham, Surrey

SIR — All these years I have lived under the impression that Middleton Bottom was a rural west-country village.

Keith White
Conford, Hampshire

SIR — Having seen her daughter's bottom and her husband's hands the subjects of eulogies in the press, poor Carol Middleton must be dreading which part of her own anatomy is to be laid out for public examination.

Philip Styles
Cheddar, Somerset

SIR — Naturally without wishing the Duchess of Cambridge any ill will, surely I am not the only person in the country who is beginning to wish that she had been born an only child?

Andrew Lilwall-Smith
Chalfont St Peter, Buckinghamshire

SIR – I find myself collecting my *Telegraph* every morning and wondering if it is a PT (Pippa Today) paper or a NPT (No Pippa Today) paper.

She's a tennis fan. Roll on Wimbledon.

Chris James
Llangernyw, Conwy

SIR – I might as well trade down to the *Sun* and save myself 65p a day if this is going to continue; at least in that paper you can see their boobs.

A.M.
Broxwood, Herefordshire

SIR – Your paper is becoming the laughing stock of the intelligentsia of Blaby.

R.M.
Blaby, Leicestershire

SIR – I had rather missed the *Daily Hurleygraph* and am pleased to note a new sense of direction with its re-branding as the *Daily Pippagraph*.

Alan Duncalf
Bampton, Devon

SIR – My wife and I are suffering withdrawal symptoms. The *Telegraph* seems to have suspended its almost daily pictures of the fragrant Samantha Cameron. Philippa Middleton is no substitute.

Michael Sandiford
Whitby, North Yorkshire

WHEN IN ONTARIO

SIR – Today I saw the Duchess of Cambridge, our future Queen of England, wearing a cowboy hat in Canada. Yes, I get the idea, but I'm still unimpressed. When we greet important visitors to Great Britain, would we like to see them sporting bowler hats or playing the bagpipes?

Cliff Tibbels
Rickmansworth, Hertfordshire

DECLINE AND FALL

SIR – Sometimes a simple piece of gossip tells so much. Take the news that Prince Harry's reputed new girlfriend, Miss Florence Brudenell-Bruce, an under-wear model, is 'a descendant of the seventh Earl of Cardigan, Lieutenant General James Thomas Brudenell, who famously led the Charge of the Light

Brigade against the Russians during the Crimean War'.

What a succinct map of the decline of western civilisation in the past 150 years.

Jillian Abbott
Whitestone, New York, USA

SIR – How sad for young Guy Pelly that he is having difficulty finding a suitable female companion to enjoy his playboy lifestyle of clubbing during the week and hunting with the Beaufort on the weekend. If only he'd lower his sights a little, I'm his gal.

C.H. (aged 57)
Valencia, Spain

SIR – If Prince Harry takes up the offer to become King of Canada then surely other members of the Commonwealth would also need a king? May I put myself forward for King of the Seychelles? I'm not sure where I sit in the pecking order for the British throne, but I did once meet Prince Philip.

Andrew Holgate
Woodley, Cheshire

THE DUKE OF EDINBURGH AT 90

SIR – The Duke of Edinburgh was 'posted'? Gad, sir. Army, RAF officers and parcels are posted; naval officers are appointed.

Adrian Holloway
Minchinhampton, Gloucestershire

SIR – I see that the Duke of Edinburgh has been given the Royal Navy. My father is 90 in December. Can he have the Royal Air Force?

Alan Mooge
Enfield, Middlesex

SIR – What a pity Her Majesty didn't appoint the Duke of Edinburgh Lord High Executioner because I have a little list . . .

Leonard Glynn
Bristol

MY FAMILY AND OTHER DOMESTIC DISASTERS

NO, I AM NOT ALRIGHT HERE!

SIR – Am I alone in being intensely irritated by shop assistants asking if I am 'alright there'? If one cannot browse in a bookshop, where can one browse?

Stores always seem to have long queues at the counter. Perhaps all the assistants are on the shop floor, inquiring after the health of their customers.

Annette Owen
Oldham, Lancashire

SIR – While purchasing a newspaper from my local Co-op this morning, the otherwise perfectly pleasant male assistant asked if I was 'having an enjoyable St Valentine's day'. As a middle-aged, middle-class, Radio 4 listener, you will anticipate the nature of my reply.

Has anyone else encountered such drivel?

Peter Wride
Westrip, Gloucestershire

SIR – I paid a recent visit to our local emporium, Trading 4U, in order to choose my wife a birthday present. At the checkout I explained that I would like the four lavatory brushes and containers to be gift-wrapped. Despite the tiresome process of having to explain that they were for my wife's birthday, I got nowhere. In fact, the checkout lady was not slow in voicing her lack of sympathy for my plight.

I do not know what to do: present them to my wife unwrapped or have a stab at wrapping them myself, despite having had no training in such matters.

To whom can a chap turn in a crisis?

John Harvey
Uckfield, East Sussex

SIR – Surely one of the most unpleasant tasks in modern life is queuing at supermarket checkouts. Eventually, a glassy-eyed assistant recites the practised words of welcome with all the enthusiasm of a very old Basset Hound. Is there not a better way?

I feel that if food shopping were predominantly a male activity and not left to the gentler, more tolerant sex, things would have already changed.

Frank Dike
Salwayash, Dorset

SIR – Standing in the queue at my local Sainsbury's the other day I was struck by a thought: there is a need for a men-only checkout.

There were several ladies in the queue in front of me. When they came to pay, all went through the same ritual: 1) Extract handbag from shopping bag; 2) Extract purse from handbag; 3) Extract credit card from purse (in one case going back into the purse to find pin number); 4) Tender card; 5) Take card and do numbers 1–3 in reverse order.

As a mere male I already had my cards in my wallet, which was in my jacket pocket.

Who invented the handbag, anyway?

Mike Usherwood
Huntington, North Yorkshire

SIR – I find it slightly irritating, when paying by plastic card at a checkout to have the displayed instructions to 'enter PIN' and 'remove card' verbally duplicated a fraction of a second earlier by the assistant. Is my wife right in telling me that I'm alone in my irritation?

John Evans
Ormskirk, Lancashire

LOVE, HONOUR AND AFFRAY

SIR – The etymology of *obey* comes from the prefix *ob*, 'facing', and *audire*, 'to listen'. In obeying her husband, a wife is simply giving him a hearing before administering a straight left.

Charles Cleall
Shaftesbury, Dorset

SIR — When I got married in 1968 my wife promised to obey. However, she always maintained that she had her fingers crossed and therefore the promise did not count. That proved to be the case.

Geoff Eley
Dunmow, Essex

OLD, ADOPTED PENSIONERS

SIR — My wife and I were thrilled to read that guidelines are now to be relaxed for 'older people to be considered for adoption'. Can anyone advise us where we can find a very rich young couple to adopt us?

R.C.
Pickering, North Yorkshire

SIR — I have discussed the prospect of adoption with my wife and she is surprisingly enthusiastic, although she said that I might be hard to place in view of my 'rather grumpy nature and habit of crackling the *Telegraph* when turning the pages'.

Chris Rome
Thruxton, Hampshire

SIR – If my wife gets to the *Telegraph* before I do, she leaves it looking as if she has slept badly in it. Is there a course I can send her on?

Patrick Brennan
Pontefract, West Yorkshire

WHEN I'M 85

SIR – Please stop printing stories about one in five of us living to be 100. If the Government gets wind of it, it'll raise the retirement age to 85.

Robin Carr
Chesham, Buckinghamshire

SIR – My husband, in his 81st year, has been successfully tossing pancakes for 60 years. And he has never worn jeans.

Caroline Ollington
Horsted Keynes, West Sussex

SIR – I am 65 years of age and despite the best efforts of my wife and daughters, I have never entered an IKEA store.

Guy Powell
Sevenoaks, Kent

SIR – How I agree with your fashion director, Hilary Alexander, that it feels good to wear pretty undies! I had just returned from town, having bought two lace bras and five pairs of frilly, lacy knickers – all at sale prices, of course, as I am a pensioner.

I may be 70, but why should the youngsters have all the fun?

Mrs Chris Gordon
Benington, Lincolnshire

SPIRIT WILLING, FLESH WEAK

SIR – I read that in Jilly Cooper's new novel *Jump,* she thought she 'ought to try to tackle elderly sex but found it very difficult'. This put me in mind of the old rhyme: *A man's not old when his hair turns grey/ Nor is he old when his teeth decay/ But a man is approaching his long last sleep/ When his mind makes appointments his body can't keep.*

John H. Davies
Buckden, North Yorkshire

SIR – As an Englishman I shake hands with male colleagues, embrace my sons and a very few other lifelong male friends. Rose-lipped and nut-brown maidens, meanwhile, get kissed on the lips. This is not always approved of by my wife but I do try to keep the practice under control.

Tony Lee-Elliott
Rothley, Leicestershire

SIR — My wife tells me she will be most pleased if a Slut Walk is planned near where we live. Although always busy, she will nonetheless find time to provide me with sandwiches, a Thermos of coffee, a camping stool and our old opera glasses so she can have the house to herself for a few hours.

Robert Vincent
Wildhern, Hampshire

SIR — While I sympathise with one of your correspondents who complains about the lack of sexy women on his morning commute, he should consider himself fortunate: I work for a company making handmade cosmetics in Poole, who seem to have a recruitment policy based on employing women each more attractive than the last.

I'm not the only one to find it hugely distracting.

Tim Palmer
Poole, Dorset

SIR – My father, who suffered the normal British reticence of his age and class, left it to my mother to tell me about the Birds and the Bees. This she did with admirable sensitivity, directness and clarity. 'And,' she added, 'I'll tell you something which your schoolfellows don't know and which will be very useful to you in the years to come: girls want it just as much as boys.'

Barry A. Kirkham
Tring, Hertfordshire

SIR – I always felt sure I had a 'mojo'. However, despite a thorough rummage behind the sofa and a perfunctory inspection of the shed, it remains elusive.

Deborah Carroll
Stockport

SIR – Michael Mosley, on the BBC's new series *Inside The Human Body*, says that most animals make it obvious when they are ready for sex. 'A cat on heat will stick her bottom in the air and go "Meow!",' he explains. 'Now most women obviously don't do this.'

It's the 'most' that makes this information so memorable. Indeed, now I know why, when I am really attracted to a woman, I invariably call her pussycat.

Huw Beynon
Llandeilo, Carmarthenshire

WELCOME, DALEY AND MICHAEL

SIR – It is with real joy that I welcome to London Daley and Michael, the first gay penguin couple to grace our city. They are a long-awaited addition to the male couples dotted around world zoos, including: New York; Bremerhaven in Germany, where in an attempt to break up the male couples, the zookeepers tried to tempt them with a few female 'scando babes' from Sweden (to no avail); and Harbin in north-east China, where the besotted couple was even allowed to get married in full Chinese tradition, wearing red shirts.

As the author of a series of fictional, illustrated books on Gus and Waldo, a couple of gay penguins in love, I'm happy I can now go and visit some real ones in my own city. The fact that there is now a new example of how love overcomes any barrier should really make us all clap our flippers with joy.

Massimo Fenati
London SW5

BATHTIME FOR BALDIES

SIR – I once read an article about a farmer whose cow lovingly licked the top of his head every morning while he fed her. Hey presto, his head, hitherto resembling a skating rink, became positively hirsute.

I immediately bought my husband a hair-scrubbing brush, it being somewhat cheaper than a cow.

Charlotte Garnett
Haslemere, Surrey

SIR – I use my wife's shower cap, and it helps keep my golden mane in impeccable condition.

Ivor Yeloff
Hethersett, Norfolk

SIR – Many men are concerned by the onset of baldness, but they should not despair; it has its uses. Today I was out walking with my wife of 48 years and was asked to remove my cap to find out whether or not it was raining. It was.

Bernard Walton
Blairgowrie, Perthshire

GARDEN FURNITURE BAN

SIR – I think I may have a remedy to the recent serious drought warnings. About two years ago, during a brainstorm, my wife purchased a small set of fairly hideous garden furniture. It does not take up too much space, so I normally keep it hidden out of sight in the shed. Every time I get it out, however, it starts raining.

Perhaps the Government could be persuaded to fund me to travel round the country with the furniture.

M.W.
Wolverley, Worcestershire

SIR – You Brits amaze me. After finally getting a spell of fine weather, you now have, according to your television news, potential hosepipe bans, increased shark sightings and more environmental pollution. Are you ever happy?

Vincent Sinnott
St Raphael, France

THE CHELSEA ART SHOW

SIR – Now that the Chelsea Flower Show seems to be more about 'installations' than flowers, why not save money and decide on the winner of the Turner Prize along with the Royal Horticultural Society awards?

Roderic Mather
Wigglesworth, North Yorkshire

SIR – Just how is one supposed to harvest the vegetables grown on a 30ft-high tower at the Chelsea Flower Show? Presumably only after having bought a ladder from B&Q, sponsors of the vegetable tower garden?

Patricia Herbert
London N5

SIR – I now realise where I am going wrong in my garden: I should throw away the lawn mower, the secateurs and the trowel. Instead, I should buy a cement mixer, some bricks and a load of timber. Then, maybe, I will get a rosette from my local council for the best garden in town.

Terry Duncan
Bridlington, East Yorkshire

I'M A BARBIE BLACKBIRD

SIR – Has anyone else got a blackbird in their garden which sings 'I'm A Barbie Girl' by Aqua?

J.S.
Exmouth, Devon

SIR – Our birds encourage me to turn each day to the *Telegraph*'s puzzles page with their SU-DO-KU cooing. After 12 hours I feel like reaching for my air rifle.

John Hague
Bishop Monkton, North Yorkshire

SIR – For the last month I have been plagued by an errant crow: the solution was an early-morning appearance in a dressing gown accompanied by Mr Webley and Scott, and his 30-inch barrels.

R.D.
Dorchester, Dorset

SIR – Soon after moving into our new home, we had a problem with a great tit pecking at a bedroom window. One day in desperation I drew a rough outline of a hawk on a piece of card and stuck it to the window. It worked.

Sheila Stone
Nafferton, East Yorkshire

SIR – I have long felt that those who interpret birdsong as spoken English are petty delusionists of the worst kind. All that changed when I was summarily addressed by a parakeet (whom I did not know) telling me quite clearly to 'F*** off'.

Considering prudence preferable to confrontation, I duly did.

Arthur W.J.G. Ord-Hume
Guildford, Surrey

GREEN (AND FISH) FINGERS

SIR – Last week my husband was in our garden watching the night-time wildlife when suddenly something fell from the sky and plopped onto the ground in front of him. He picked it up . . . it was a warm fish finger. We are seeking some explanation.

Valerie Hampton
Tettenhall, West Midlands

SIR – Am I the only one to notice that my garden flora seems to be adapting itself to the fortnightly collections of my brown bin? Whenever the bin is full, the grass puts on an extra spurt and develops a sort of smug look about it.

Has any research been done on this?

Nick Tracken
Welwyn, Hertfordshire

SIR – I was taken by your article about talking to inanimate objects to encourage them to grow. My wife goes one stage further: on regular tours of the garden no words are uttered, but under-performing plants receive a red woollen bow to indicate that, unless they try harder, it's the compost bin for them.

She's had a 100 per cent success rate so far – an outstanding result for what we call 'the yarn of shame'.

A.G.
Bradfield, Devon

SIR – I'm losing my wife of longstanding to Monty Don – blast him. He can turn over a yard of soil with a flick of his wrist, differentiate between a flower and a weed, and propagate.

I will not plant out my asparagus this weekend – I will play golf, so there!

Malcolm Allen
Berkhamsted, Hertfordshire

SIR – I think there should be a prize awarded for innovation to the gentleman I am watching blowing the snow off his car and clearing the driveway with a leaf-blower. It is remarkably efficient.

Frances Dodwell
Idsworth Down, Hampshire

SIR – For any keen gardener who has completed the census online, and is concerned about how to dispose of the unwanted forms, might I suggest that they use them to line their runner-bean trench; they are the perfect size.

Ted Shorter
Tonbridge, Kent

LIVELY CENSUS DEBATES

SIR – The recent census has prompted a lively debate in my household. Question 19 asks, 'How well can you speak English?' My wife believes that her English parents and upbringing entitle her to claim she speaks English 'very well'. However, having observing that, among other errors, she often uses *less* when she means *fewer*, and frequently confuses *averse* and *adverse*, I have entered her as speaking English merely 'well'.

Do you agree with her that I am being overly pernickety?

Robert Wilson
Broxbourne, Hertfordshire

SIR – 'How well can you speak English?' asks the form. Compared to whom?

John Maloney
Biggar, Lanarkshire

SIR – The census is likely to shift the balance of power within a number of households. My wife is now Person Two.

Jeremy Leigh Pemberton
Sittingbourne, Kent

SIR – I assume my surname fitted. My wife, who completed the form, did not tell me otherwise.

Piers Casimir-Mrowczynski
Gustard Wood, Hertfordshire

SIR – As the owner of a three-bed semi in an affluent village in rural Wiltshire, I am aghast to learn that in this year's census, two of my three young sons are to be labelled under-privileged because they share a bedroom.

James Hawkins
Whiteparish, Wiltshire

BOMBS (AND FATHERS) AWAY!

SIR – I was somewhat bemused to read of the extension to paid paternity leave. When my first-born was due, I left my wife alone at a maternity home about 200 miles from her nearest relatives and hurried off to Met briefing before two trips at a night fighter Operational Conversion Unit. I was somewhere between 40,000 and 50,000 feet when he was born.

Visiting hours were strict and policed by Matron. I did manage a short evening visit before night flying again.

No chance of some retrospective leave (pay), I suppose?

John Hyland
Aylesbury, Buckinghamshire

SIR – Paternity Leave? It may be fashionable in the Southern Counties, but in North Yorkshire, I can assure you that bringing up babies is regarded as women's work. Real men would never have any involvement.

Ian Gill
Great Ouseburn, North Yorkshire

SIR – Surely the prime benefit of having been born a bastard is that one has no need to indulge in the recently imported, alien 'celebration' of Father's Day.

John Letchford
Elsenham, Hertfordshire

BOURNE ULTIMATUM

SIR — Perhaps Carolyn Bourne, formidable writer of the famous mother-in-law email, could be persuaded to expand her email into a handy booklet containing more guidance for our youth, including the correct usage of the word *like*.

D.M.
Horley, Surrey

SIR — As a mother-in-law in training, I am fortunate to be blessed with two lovely and well-mannered daughters-in-law. However, if it were not so, and I wished to write as did Carolyn Bourne, I would do so by handwritten letter, on headed notepaper. Such bad form to use email.

Sarah Rushmere
Upper Beeding, West Sussex

SIR — Despite much provocation, my mother-in-law has never put pen to paper to instruct me on my many failings. If she has ever felt the need to say such things, she has always bitten her tongue, unlike her daughter.

Timothy Shucksmith
Lovedean, Hampshire

SIR – Could Carolyn Bourne be persuaded to send one of her mother-in-law emails to Sally Bercow?

Roger Balchin
Horsell, Surrey

FINED BY THE FASHION FUZZ

SIR – Surely it is time for the fashion among teenage boys of wearing trousers that barely cover their thighs – let alone their backsides – to be consigned to the dustbin?

Don't they realise how ridiculous they look? Why can't we have fashion police – authorised to hand out tickets to those whose attire is an affront to good taste?

Robert Readman
Bournemouth, Dorset

SIR – There was a time when ladies of all ages got out their summer frocks and skirts at this time of year, thus gladdening the hearts of us men. And yet while walking down my local high street this afternoon in bright sunshine, I noticed that all the ladies were wearing trousers. Should I blame the fashion industry? Or is Surrey just really boring?

M.F.
Cobham, Surrey

SIR – When shopping last week in Rusthall, a village suburb of Tunbridge Wells, I noted that of the 61 women who passed the baker's shop during my 10 minutes therein, 59 were wearing trousers. The two who sported frocks were over 50 years old.

M.R.B.
Rusthall, Kent

SIR – I have never worn trousers. My elderly aunts considered them an unseemly mode of dress for a well brought-up young lady.

Bunty Richings
Windlesham, Surrey

SIR – I'm a not-unattractive female in her mid-twenties. For me, the sexiest part of a man's body is his legs. Why, then, do current men's fashions dictate foisting upon their wearers those ugly 'shorts' that extend to well below the knee, in the process ruining the superb physiognomic curve of the male leg?

The result is nothing short of laughable – and the biggest turn-off imaginable. Faced with such an off-putting fashion disaster, a man-free existence in a nunnery seems preferable.

Yours in utter desperation,

Annette Hunt
Datchet, Berkshire

SIR – Even though I am now over 60, I have, with a great deal of help and advice from my wife and children, tried to dress both smartly and reasonably fashionably. My fashion world therefore fell apart this morning when I saw on your front page one of my favourite shirts being modelled by Jeremy Clarkson.

Richard Dalgleish
Kingsclere, Berkshire

SIR – Does anyone know why manufacturers persist in putting the chafing side of a seam on the inside of socks and men's underpants?

Barrie Yelland
Helston, Cornwall

INVOLUNTARY EUTHANASIA

SIR – I read your headline, 'Help 60,000 more to die at home' in some alarm. Now, having stocked up on food and drink, and chained and bolted the front door, my wife and I sit here, refusing to answer the bell and hoping for the best.

David Salter
Kew, Surrey

SIR – I see no reason why we should ask the terminally ill how they want to die. According to the death notices in our local newspaper, at least nine out of ten state that the person died 'peacefully'.

Mike McDowell
Cam Green, Gloucestershire

SIR – If so many of us are going to die early because of obesity and alcohol, how is it that income from annuities continues to fall?

Martin Harvey
Eastbourne, East Sussex

SIR – If we are to be given a choice of how we die, I think I shall opt for drowning in a butt of malmsey, but I would be happy to settle for port.

Peter Howell
Malmesbury, Wiltshire

ALCOHOLIC INSANITY

SIR – I note that the Royal Society of Psychiatrists has suggested that the recommended limit on alcohol consumption for over-65s should be reduced drastically to about half a pint of beer a day. Could this be an attempt on the part of the society to drum up more business? After all, it's the couple of pints I consume every lunchtime which keep me sane.

David L.G. Hallowell
Walton-on-the-Hill, Surrey

SIR – Anyone who accepts the job title of Chairman of Older People's Substance Misuse Working Group should visit a psychiatrist.

Terence O'Flynn
West Lavington, Wiltshire

SIR – Eleven units of alcohol per seven-day week? No rational mind produced that ratio; the only thing that unites the two numbers is that both are primes. And if we extrapolate to a 30-day month, we get 47 units, another prime. The author of this policy should seek psychiatric help over his obsession with prime numbers.

Peter Urben
Kenilworth, Derbyshire

SIR – I am nearing my 80th birthday, and no one will tell me what I should or should not drink. My wife and I have a glass or two of wine every night with our evening meal. The idea is not to arrive at the Pearly Gates looking a million dollars, but to be waving a glass of Merlot in one hand and a bar of chocolate in the other, saying, 'Whoopee, what a ride!'

Tony Woodcock
Stoke on Trent, Staffordshire

SIR – My wife and I have only one word for the experts on geriatric alcohol abuse: Horlicks!

Phil Higginbotham
Chesterfield, Derbyshire

SIR – I see that, according to the Bishop of Stafford, alcohol abuse is one of the major sins of our time. A while back, a parishioner gave me a tea towel displaying this poem:

He who drinks gets drunk;
He who gets drunk goes to sleep;
He who goes to sleep does not sin;
He who does not sin goes to heaven.
So let's all get drunk and go to heaven!
Clearly the Bishop has a different flock to mine.

Rev. Duncan Lloyd-James
Seaford, East Sussex

UNHEALTHY SAFETY

SIR – My daughter was recently informed that her son, aged seven, would not be allowed to participate in school swimming lessons because his shorts had a pocket in them. After a risk assessment, it had been decided there was a potential danger that another child might get a foot caught in the offending pocket. How ridiculous is that?

William Colston
Bingham, Nottinghamshire

SIR – I have just bought a pack of dental floss from Marks & Spencer. On the back there is a number to ring 'in case of emergency'. I am living in fear now. What peril lies hidden in this innocent-looking pack?

> **Mrs T. Repper**
> Sheffield

SIR – My complimentary hotel shampoo bottle gave the warning 'Avoid eye contact'. Try as I might, I couldn't help staring straight at it two or three times during my shower.

> **David Readman**
> Leigh-on-Sea, Essex

SIR – One of the many disappointments with this Government is that they have yet to tackle this poison in our society. I don't think I am alone in wincing when I see workers digging up the road wearing hard hats. Do they expect aircraft parts to drop on them, or perhaps a meteorite?

> **Sid Davies**
> Bramhall, Cheshire

SIR – Common sense is so rare in our society today. Should it not be renamed? Sensible suggestions would be appreciated.

Robert Guttridge
Sheffield

AN ENGLISHMAN'S HOME

SIR – Ken Clarke says I can now stab burglars. That's fine, but it leaves blood all over the carpets. Can I electrocute them instead?

Robert Warner
West Woodhay, Berkshire

POLITICS: THE ART OF THE IMPOSSIBLE

THE STUDENTS ARE REVOLTING

SIR – I can't get excited about these students protesting. Compared to the first and second Grosvenor Square demonstrations in 1968, this lot are pussycats. Most of the students who travelled to London with me in 1968 got arrested, injured or laid, and in some cases, all three.

Kids today don't know they're born (and the summers were hotter).

Philip Saunders
Ditchingham Dam, Suffolk

SIR – I have just two words to say on the subject: water cannon. The cost would be low, because there would be no shortage of volunteers to man them free of charge. In my case, I would even pay for the privilege.

Guy Rose
London SW14

SIR – May I suggest if the police are to use water cannon to disperse rioting students, they include some soap in the tank?

Finlay Mason
Luxembourg

SIR – If only a substance could be added to the water that attracted those extremely clever little sniffer dogs. Why not essence of cannabis, for instance, which would make identification a lot easier?

I.A.
Kellas, Moray

SIR – Perhaps the use of drift nets, fired from cannons, such as used to trap wildfowl for ringing, could be an effective method of rounding up groups of rioters?

Robert Stewart
Maurens, France

SIR – Might I suggest that the police combine the technologies of SmartWater identification and paintballing? I do not think it beyond their capabilities to come up with a more powerful delivery system that would soak the offenders' clothing and skin with easily identifiable genetic markers. The system could remain active for 28 days, so that criminals who evade immediate detection could be picked up at a later date.

The rioters could always divest themselves of any incriminating clothing, but it would be somewhat difficult to riot when naked.

Paul Chesters
Wallsey, Wirral

... BUT SO IS HALF THE COUNTRY

SIR — None of the discussion about the recent widespread riots has mentioned that rioting and smashing things up is fun. When the blood's up and you're running in the herd, the darker side of animal instincts is ready to take over.

The challenge, therefore, is to create a suitable policy to outweigh this. Three years' military service on conviction for rioting should do it.

If the idea of the Army is too much for you (or for the Army), then three applications of the Taser at monthly intervals might also have a modestly effective outcome.

We don't need to bring back the birch.

J.C.
Great Malvern, Worcestershire

SIR — As a magistrate of 30 years' service I often wish I had had the sentencing powers in a science fiction book I once read, in which the miscreant was beamed into the Middle Ages to undergo the stocks.

Adrian Holloway
Minchinhampton, Gloucestershire

54

SIR – The time has surely come for Jeremy Kyle to take his place as youth minister.

Kathy Heuvel
Mickleham, Surrey

SIR – I know this is very simplistic but the police began to lose control of the streets when they gave up prosecuting people riding bicycles at night without lights. This clearly sent a signal that the law could be broken with impunity at all levels.

J.F. Collins
Groby, Leicestershire

SIR – Here, in Crickhowell, we had our own version of the recent riots. A local resident commented to me, grumpily, that the emptying of garden waste bins could often be late. I agreed with him, equally grumpily.

Strangely it wasn't covered by the media.

Phil Bailey (social delinquent)
Crickhowell, Powys

SIR — People will say I am out of touch, but surely all this rioting and looting will stop when the perpetrators head for the moors tomorrow for the start of the grouse-shooting season?

Nicky Samengo-Turner
Hundon, Suffolk

SIR — Instead of 'moving on' from the recent riots, why not embrace them in next year's athletic extravaganza? Here are some examples: synchronised looting, the modern kleptathlon and Olympic torching. Or even forget the whole thing and concentrate on rebuilding our country.

Professor Rex Last
New Alyth, Perthshire

SIR — In spite of the riots in our towns and cities, I didn't see any looters nicking a duck house.

Valda Mossman
Newlyn, Cornwall

. . . AND SO, OF COURSE, ARE THE POLITICIANS

SIR – In the last few days, while watching BBC Parliament, I have observed in the House of Commons chamber: a lady filing her nails, a gentleman yawning repeatedly and a front bench spokesman apparently chewing. Is this behaviour acceptable, particularly following the expenses scandal?

H.W.
Lesbury, Northumberland

SIR – I have just used my credit card for the first time at John Lewis. Does this qualify me to be an MP?

Norma Goodwin
Saighton, Cheshire

SIR – Anyone prepared to be seen in public sporting a tie tied so appallingly as Elliot Morley's is clearly not to be trusted. He has the appearance of an elderly schoolboy and the tie in question looks like some unfortunate corporate affair, probably a freebie.

Duncan Cavenagh
Director, Cavenagh Ties
Kingston upon Thames, Surrey

SIR — Ed Miliband has pledged to make the Labour Party 'the party of the grafters'. He's a bit behind the times; three Labour MPs are already in prison for graft.

Ted Hawkins
Sandhurst, Berkshire

SIR — One cannot imagine why prisoners should crave voting rights when we seem to be sending them a regular supply of politicians to share among themselves.

George Langton
Southsea, Hampshire

EMPEROR DAVE PIN-UP

SIR — Has anyone else noticed the striking resemblance of David Cameron's Bullingdon portrait to the young Napoleon Bonaparte? And can I be the only woman to find our Prime Minister, in this guise, a better pin-up than Colin Firth?

Please could you print a larger version?

Madeline Helps
Norton St Philip, Somerset

SIR — The refusal of a waitress to serve coffee to David Cameron while he was on holiday in Tuscany should cause alarm at the Foreign Office. Are they not aware of his earlier active membership of the Bullingdon Club? I would object strongly if the Government purse had to pay for any ensuing damage.

Bryan Smalley
Much Hadham, Hertfordshire

SIR — How pleasant to see a picture of our Prime Minister relaxing on a family holiday in Ibiza. Not a glance at the lady sunbathing topless next to him. Good man — I'm sure Samantha approved.

Geoffrey Aldridge
Wingrave, Buckinghamshire

CLEGG AND OTHER CALAMITIES

SIR — I think it a little unfair to berate Nick Clegg for forgetting he was running the country in the Prime Minister's absence; after all, everyone else did.

Derrick Pepperell
Cheltenham, Gloucestershire

SIR – Hilaire Belloc anticipated Nick Clegg with his satire on Lord Lundy, who 'was too freely moved to tears'. It must surely be only a matter of time before he is sent to govern New South Wales.

Alasdair Macleod
Newton Poppleford, Devon

SIR – Nick Clegg says he just puts on music and cries. I don't even need the music; I just think of misled politicians ruining our landscape with wind farms.

Celia Hobbs
Penicuik, Midlothian

SIR – They say that we eventually start to resemble our pets, but it seems that Chris Huhne's unpredictability, instability and uncontrollability is already mimicking his much-loved wind turbines.

Brian Christley
Abergele, Conwy

SIR – Am I alone in looking forward to when a politician does 'something right' rather than 'nothing wrong'?

Vivien Seymour
Marlow, Buckinghamshire

SIR – After nine months of a coalition government, am I alone in thinking that Gordon Brown, Alistair Darling et al. seem far less incompetent in retrospect?

Bruce Chalmers
Goring-by-sea, West Sussex

SIR – David Cameron likes to describe his distinctly average ministers as 'superb', 'excellent', 'exemplary' and so on. If he should ever appoint a genuinely able minister I wonder what superlatives he will have left to use.

David Saunders
Sidmouth, Devon

THE NUCLEAR GUNPOWDER PLOT

SIR – Vince Cable bears a striking resemblance to Guy Fawkes. It must be something to do with the hat. I wonder if he will suffer a similar fate.

David Ellis
Tarves, Aberdeenshire

SIR – Don't overestimate Vince Cable. His only real political ambition has been to get a railway carriage to himself.

Malcolm Parkin
Kinnesswood, Kinross

NO SMOKE WITHOUT FIRE

SIR – Alan Milburn is quite wrong about Nye Bevan 'turning in his grave' about the proposed NHS reforms. As a young lad I attended Nye's cremation – at the newly opened Croesyceiliog Crematorium.

P.R.
Gwent

THE HUGE SOCIETY

SIR – The Big Society is here now. I saw some of its representatives waddling out of a fast food shop today.

Malcolm Allen
Berkhamsted, Hertfordshire

SIR – There is no such thing as Big Society.

Andrew Casey
Epsom, Surrey

SIR – Will the Government be communicating with us through the *Big Issue*?

Peter J.L. de Snoo
Perranwell, Cornwall

SIR –
    'Big Society is my mission'.
    A Cherie Booth phrase.
    Because it is 'Poor English'.
    Like 'Fit For Purpose'.
    MY.
    MISSION.
    NO.
    You little 'Twot'.
    Your MISSION.

Is to run the United Kingdom.
Your PERSONAL 'Mission'.
Is 'reserved' for the pulpit of 'Holy Trinity
Brompton'.
You are NOT to abuse the trust placed in you as
'PM' by 'getting back' at Britain for the buggery
you suffered at Eton by pursuing the known
'destructive' policy of 'Big Society'.
So it's all going to 'end in tears' here, isn't it?
PRIME MINISTER.
YES.
cc UK Records
Buckingham Palace
BIG BROTHER
British State Security ('B.O.S.S.')
GCHQ
22 SAS
'The Circus'

M

TURBULENT PRIESTS

SIR — The Archbishop of Canterbury has criticised the Government's policies 'for which no one voted'. May I remind Dr Williams that we did not vote for him either, and that since Ant and Dec have a wider constituency than he does, I hold his views in lesser esteem.

Neil Truelove
Clifton, Bedfordshire

SIR — A man who cannot control his own eyebrows has no business telling the Prime Minister what to do.

Jan Alcock
Stonyhurst, Lancashire

SIR — Why is David Cameron pussyfooting around as usual? Surely his Chief Whip could find four Conservative backbenchers willing to arm themselves with sub-machine pistols and rid us of this turbulent priest?

Peter Croft
Cambridge

RUM, SODOMY AND THE DEVIL

SIR – Call me a religious maniac if you will, but I believe the first step in recovering the Royal Navy from its current situation should be to rescind the decision made in 2004 to permit devil worship in one, at least, of HM Ships.

Since then we've had the Iranians capturing our sailors, Somali pirates capturing Mr and Mrs Chandler and the RAF selling off what might have been our last hope of deploying fixed-wing aircraft over the next 10 years.

Lieutenant Commander M.P. Toolan (retd.)
Chelmsford, Essex

SIR – Congratulations, Dave. No Harriers, no *Ark Royal*. No hope for the young, save those lucky enough to read history and reflect on the days when Britain's name meant something in world circles.

Today Britain scrapes around in the rocky mist of uncertainty, feeling her way through choking clouds of fuliginous murk hoisted upon us by a fainéant band of European contriculators [sic].

Meanwhile, we career towards a dominant role in health and safety: cutting-edge computer crash helmets for fat little boys and fat little girls perchance they fall off their sedentary perch. Rubber ladders, rubber hammers, rubber paving and rubber cars so that we can all safely bump around until we're finally . . . rubbed out altogether.

Joe Gibson Dawson
Withnell, Lancashire

SYMPATHY FOR THE DEVIL

SIR – I could not help but be drawn to the alluring picture of Carole Caplin under the caption 'I didn't sleep with Blair' on the front page of today's paper. For the very first time I felt sorry for Tony, but don't worry, the feeling soon passed.

David Chillistone
Portishead, Somerset

SIR – I haven't slept with Tony Blair either, but I have sure as hell been f***** by him.

Robert Dobson
Seal, Kent

SIR – I am not in the least surprised by Cherie Blair's latest revelation that her dear husband still sets her pulses racing. The mere mention of his name takes my blood pressure to dangerous levels.

Victor Bethell
Tunbridge Wells, Kent

SIR – Yet another divulgence of personal information from our former Prime Minister's wife! This brings to mind a Polish proverb a friend translated for me: 'The cow that moos the loudest rarely gives any milk'.

Dr Stephanie Susay
Cuffley, Hertfordshire

SIR – There is a pithy West Country saying which goes, 'There be them as says and them as does'.

Geoff Dyke
Longfield, Kent

SIR– Perhaps it's a figment of my fevered imagination, but Larry the cat seems to have a similar smirk that graced the face of that former Downing Street resident, Tony Blair.

Ivor Yeloff
Hethersett, Norfolk

SIR – I thought it was Tony Blair who had the dicky heart and his pal, Bill Clinton, the opposite.

Luke Grant
Pensax Common, Worcestershire

HE'S BEHIND YOU!

SIR – I do wish politicians would stop wearing make-up. In your front-page photograph of George Osborne, he looks like a pantomime dame.

Raymon Doyle
Bearwood, Dorset

PEN FRIEND

SIR – Broadcast on the *10 O'Clock News* this evening was a film report which showed the Foreign Secretary retiring into his diplomatic car following his Libya meeting with the French President. William Hague duly proceeded to mark his briefing notes with a rather cheap-looking, blue ballpoint pen.

Even in a time of austere measures, I believe the Treasury could afford to provide him with a more superior writing tool for the job. I happen to have available a rather nice classic black-and-gold-finish

Parker 51 vintage fountain pen, if the FCO is interested.

Andrew Porter
Harleston, Suffolk

GOING IN TO BAT FOR HAGUE

SIR – William Hague and Christopher Myers shared a room when campaigning during the last election. So what? During the Himbleton Village Cricket team tour of Barnstaple, April 2009, I shared a room with Martyn Preece. However, that didn't mean we both batted for the other side.

Ben Sinclair
Bentley, Worcestershire

SIR – I shared a room with 49 other males when I was at school; it was called a dormitory.

Anthony (straight) Messenger
Windsor, Berkshire

SIR – As a conscript I shared my 'bedroom' with 27 other young men – was the war won by an army of homosexuals?

> **R. Edgar Jones**
> Penrhyn Bay, Conwy

SIR – While serving in Gibraltar during the Second World War, I shared a room with a fellow sergeant for several months. On the day Brussels was liberated, I shared a double bed with a Northumberland fusilier (it's a long story); my wife was quite happy that it was not with an enthusiastic amateur.

At the first reunion after the war, held at the Savoy hotel (7th Armoured division), two officers booked a double room. Later, some of us missed the last train home to Devon. We finished up three in a double bed and two on the floor.

Happy days!

> **J.C.C.**
> MTO 2nd Bn.
> Devonshire Regiment

SIR – It is not the allegations surrounding William Hague and his special advisor that I find extraordinary, but the fact that it is felt that the 25-year-old Chris Myers, on a salary of £30,000, has any useful advice to offer the Foreign Secretary.

At 25, I was in no position to offer a Secretary of State any advice of any worth. Now at the age of 51, I feel I have a number of pieces of advice for any cabinet ministers who would wish to listen. These are not, however, printable in the letters page of a leading daily newspaper.

S.P.
Headcorn, Kent

REPATRIATING THE SCOTS

SIR – Am I alone in favouring a move towards Scottish Independence? Think of the advantages: different time zones, a reduction in unemployment as we rebuild Hadrian's Wall, this time with barbed wire and searchlights on the top, and most importantly of all, the compulsory repatriation of all Scots living in England.

There is one woman in my office for whom I would gladly turn out on the platform at King's Cross to ensure she got on the train.

Paul Phillips
New Barnet, Hertfordshire

SIR – Briefly, please. What is the point of Scotland?

John A. Jones
Sketty, Swansea

SIR – Will you please stop publishing letters
pointing out that the English would be very happy to
be rid of Scotland. It's true, but if the Scots get wind
of it, they'll cling on forever.

M.B.
Beckenham, Kent

VERY ALTERNATIVE VOTING

SIR – The suggestion that a few more topics might be
added to the list for decision by referendum in May
is a first-class opportunity. Apart from the obvious
one – should Britain leave the EU? – how about a
ban on professional football?

Nicholas Wightwick
Rossett, Cheshire

SIR – Perhaps we could be asked on the AV ballot
paper: 'Which Johnny would you like your laws
decided by: English or Foreigner?'

Jonathan Fulford
Bosham, West Sussex

SIR – For some years now I have had a dream in
which Her Majesty the Queen, dressed in full Garter
robes and holding aloft a sword, is driven down the
Mall in a tank by Lord Tebbit. She declares that
Britain is to leave the EU. Millions cheer her on her
proud procession, waving Union flags.

Daniel Deasy
Oxford

SIR – Before we consider using AV for Parliamentary
elections, shouldn't we test it out in the Eurovision
Song Competition?

Neil Asher
Mountsorrel, Leicestershire

SIR – If Nick Clegg can share the reins of power
under the present voting system, it is not a change to
the system we need, but an alternative to democracy.

Andrew Courtney
Hampton Wick, Middlesex

SIR – Anyone who can vote for Princess Diana as the third-greatest Briton ever to have lived should be barred from voting in political elections.

Sandy Pratt
Lingfield, Surrey

SIR – I noticed that there were only two options on the AV ballot paper: Yes or No. What happened to 'Good God, No'?

Ralph Griffiths
New Malden, Surrey

SIR – I voted 1 for No and 2 for Yes, just to prove I understood the system.

Alan E. Quaife
Loughton, Essex

SIR – I find it difficult enough to pick one candidate in an election, let alone three.

N.P. Scott
Harpenden, Hertfordshire

SIR – I sampled the UK referendum debate through satellite television, hoping that it would equal the passion of Britain's Reform Bill crisis of 1831–32, and emulate the cogency of New Zealand's national seminar on voting reform in 1992–93.

Alas, all I caught was an advertisement for the Yes campaign, which showed how AV could help 10 insipid young people decide whether to go to a pub or a coffee bar. Surely they could have found a pub that served coffee?

Professor Ged Martin
Youghal, County Cork, Ireland

SPIN DANDY

SIR – Your photograph of the gadget-clad Craig Oliver, the new communications chappy at No. 10, led me to conclude that the spirit of dandyism is alive and well – although it could be said that I'm not that well qualified to judge such matters, being an oldish (73) and scruffy cyclist.

I'd like to know, however, how he carries all this equipment on his bicycle. We should be informed; after all he is the communications chappy.

John Curry
Harlow, Essex

SIR – While Mr Oliver may have all the requisite gear of the very modern PR, he seems to have forgotten his cufflinks. Not even iPads have an app to fasten your shirtsleeves.

William McMullan
London N7

OFF WITH HIS ED

SIR – If Ed Balls was part of a plot to make Gordon Brown prime minister then, at the very least, he should be charged with high treason.

Michael Duhig
Bishops Stortford, Hertfordshire

SIR – I recently changed to your newspaper for a greater level of erudition. Imagine my distress, therefore, on finding that the first five and a half pages of today's issue were full of Balls.

Graham Peters
Bodiam, East Sussex

SIR – I would just like to reassure the Prime Minister that he is not alone in finding Ed Balls the most annoying person in modern politics.

Stefan Reynolds
Godalming, Surrey

SIR – Am I alone in wondering why Harridan Harpy person's every action makes me want to kick the cat and bugger the missus? Her sanctimonious features resemble a half-starved rat peering through a bale of hay.

Andreas Wright
Bessines-sur-Gartempe, France

MATT'S MILIBAND

SIR – Is it unkind of me that the more I see and hear Ed Miliband, the more I begin to wonder if he was designed by Matt Pritchett?

Harry Smith
Welwyn Garden City, Hertfordshire

SIR – We should send good wishes to Ed Miliband that he makes a speedy recovery from the operation on his nose. Let us also hope that when he wakes up, he does not sound like Gordon Brown.

David Heath
Westcliff-on-Sea, Essex

SIR – I presume your report on Labour's street party celebrations for 'Ed and Justine's' wedding was an April Fool – and in bad taste at that; it made me feel physically sick. However, there is no mention of it today. Please put me out of my agony.

Carolyn Hill
Burbage, Wiltshire

SIR – Who does Mr Edward Miliband think he is? Royalty? I thank God he is NOT.

S.R.
Warsop, Nottinghamshire

SIR – While I am pleased to see that Edward Miliband is making an honest woman of Justine Thornton, he is still no gentleman. If he were, he would know that he should be on the outside of the pavement in your picture today.

Jonathan L. Kelly
Yatton, Somerset

SIR – Ed Miliband getting married? He'll be pronouncing his 't's next.

Charles Vandepeer
Blean, Kent

THE USE AND ABUSE OF LANGUAGE

THREATENING PHRASES

SIR – Am I alone in feeling vaguely threatened when people tell me to 'take care'?

A.H.N. Gray
Edinburgh

SIR – Are my wife and I the only ones who find extremely annoying the current habit of being told to 'Enjoy!' every course served by a waiter or waitress?

John Harvey
Budleigh Salterton, Devon

SIR – Can any of your readers suggest what *occasional* tables do for the rest of the time?

Stephen Jerrams
Stockport, Cheshire

SIR – Please could someone tell me where the word *sitting* has disappeared to? Everyone now says things like, 'I was sat on a wall'.

Perhaps it's the effort of getting those extra four letters out. Mind you, very few people have a sitting room anymore, so maybe that has something to do with it.

Phil Birkett
Standlake, Oxfordshire

SIR – A new word seems to have crept into the language of sport in recent weeks: *stand-out*. Apart from the fact that it is three letters longer (ignoring the hyphen), why has *outstanding* fallen out of favour?

Roger Peart
Wimborne, Dorset

SIR – Hyphens are very important. I remember a phrase from my schooldays, a long time ago: 'When she heard the remark, she had that fellow-feeling in her breast.'

H. Nairn
Ashtead, Surrey

PRESENT IMPERFECT

SIR – I wonder why academics use the so-called historical present tense, e.g. 'Napoleon marches on Moscow'. I find this affectation distracting ever since I am at school in the 1960s.

Sam Kelly
Dobcross, Lancashire

SIR – I read more and more about people who have events taking place 'on their watch'. From where does

one acquire such a wondrous timepiece? All mine
does is tell me the time.

Gerald Fisher
Kettering, Northamptonshire

LOST IN TRANSLATION

SIR – The story about a councillor being warned for
using the word *faggots* reminded me of my first trip to
the USA while working for a tobacco company.
When asked at a social occasion what I did, I replied,
'I flog fags.'

I was soon informed that this had a different
meaning in the USA.

Richard Duncan
Guildford, Surrey

P.S. Hopefully this will get through your email filter.

SIR – While on parking duty today at our church for
Royal Ascot I was asked by two well-dressed
gentlemen where the 'comfort room' was. I showed
them our two Portaloos. I hope they found them
suitably 'comfortable'.

Duncan Rayner
Sunningdale, Berkshire

SIR – I never cease to be amazed by how many people say 'the hoi polloi' when they want to refer to 'the upper crust', whereas the Greek term *hoi polloi* means the many, the masses.

It may, of course, be an orchestrated move to reverse its meaning, rather like *wicked*, which now means 'rather good' in the *lingua franca*.

Ken Freeman
Willaston, Wirral

SIR – While trying to obtain a quote for car insurance from an overseas call centre, my husband was accused of using a profanity. His crime? In response to a question about his health, he had replied, 'I'm fit 'n' well.'

Try saying it quickly with a Yorkshire accent.

Joy Leach
Peterlee, County Durham

PROFANE DELIGHT

SIR – Being on the receiving end of an expletive can be an uplifting experience. Yesterday evening, my wife and I, on leaving a Chelsea eaterie were overtaken on the pavement by a young woman blithely shouting obscenities into her mobile phone. I remonstrated with a comment about her

'charming' language and was subjected to the riposte:
'And you can f*** off, you posh ****!'

After 30 years in exile from the North, this was
the first time I had been accused of being posh.

S. Barker
East Grinstead, West Sussex

SIR – I am always surprised when historical serials on
the BBC use the word *pregnant* in dialogue. Surely this
was never used back then? Until the 1960s or 1970s,
people always said things like 'expecting', sometimes
followed by 'in the family way', or 'having a happy
event'.

I doubt if a rather genteel lady in Candleford
would even have heard of the word. It would have
sounded like someone was swearing.

Stella Henley
St Helier, Jersey

SIR – Why is that women have hen (bird) parties and
men have a stag (mammal) and not a cock (bird)
party?

Dr P.W.M. Copeman
The Athenaeum, London SW1

SIR – My experience suggests that there is not a casual acceptance of the most offensive word in the English language. I coach a group of young (18–30) athletes drawn from all parts of the country. When one of the lads used the dreaded word – inadvertently, I suspect – the outraged girls practically lynched him.

George Edwards
Mumbles, Swansea

THE DAILY BASIS TELEGRAPH

SIR – Yet again the phrase 'on a daily basis' appears in your paper. Your sub-editors are not doing their jobs if they fail to shorten it. *Daily* is quite sufficient and leaves more room for real news.

Ray Dransfield
Seaston, Cornwall

SIR – Can I vote 'as the recession bites' as the most overused press phrase of the past two years?

A.P.
Lamberhurst, Kent

SIR – Am I alone in being appalled by your decision to publish the expression 'get your ass in gear' in a letter by Admiral Sir John Woodward? Rather than that lamentable Americanism, you should have deployed the good old English word *arse*.

For shame, sir!

Professor Chris Barton
Longton, Staffordshire

SIR – I relished the last sentence in one of the letters published yesterday; the correct use of the plural of emporium was heart-warming. Good man!

Dr Russell Steele
Exeter, Devon

SIR – I was amazed to read in your report that 'the US Navy Seals made the final decision to kill bin Laden rather than the President'.

Paul Abbott
Hove, East Sussex

SIR – I bought *The Daily Telegraph Style Guide* by Simon Heffer. One was reassured that, even if all others succumbed, at least your journal would always use the proven and tested *railway station* to denote a place where one joined a train service.

Alas, your report entitled 'Rail Fares Booming' shows that even this was a forlorn hope; we are all now apparently doomed to join such a service at a *train station*.

David Pearson
Haworth, West Yorkshire

SIR – I am intrigued to be informed that, 'Your Telegraph vouchers are in the post and should be arriving with you by June 21'. How can they arrive with me if I am already here?

On the bright side, I should be grateful that the vouchers will not – in train speak – *be arriving into me*. That would be even more painful.

Dr C.D.E. Morris
Walsall, West Midlands

SIR – I fully appreciate the need for the *Telegraph* to be at the cutting edge of gender equality by allowing the fairer sex to report on cricket – even on Test Matches – but when your female correspondent discusses the international grounds being in the 'throws' of expensive rebuilding works, she is obviously thinking about soft furnishings.

This may have some relevance at Lord's or the Oval, but not at Cardiff, surely?

Brian Simpson
Churchinford, Somerset

SIR — I try to remain loyal to the *Telegraph* but you have really gone too far with your front-page reference to Steven Davies, 'becoming the first serving professional cricketer to publicly out himself'. What kind of English is that supposed to be? It is bad enough creating such an ugly split infinitive, but what sort of verb is to 'out oneself'?

I do not expect a newspaper like the *Telegraph* to resort to such jive talk.

Charles E.J. Boston FRICS
London SW3

GRATING PRONOUNCIATIONS

SIR — A new word has crept into the English language, having been introduced by Nick Clegg during the election, taken up by Ed Balls recently, and even used by George Osborne on the radio this morning.

We now *crate* new laws, or *crate* unemployment. Will someone please tell them to put the E back where it belongs before we all start to *procrate* the next generation?

Pamela Le Bailly
Kilkhampton, Cornwall

SIR – I never thought I would see the day a Conservative Chancellor used the expression 'one pence'. Can we now expect him to refer every *Febuary* to his *Seketary*, who is *vunerable*? Is it too late to send him to a proper grammar school? At least Dennis Skinner never pretends to have been educated.

It is bad enough having television presenters use these excruciating words.

Allan Sims
West Chiltington, West Sussex

SIR – I find it most uncanny that the BBC now refers to 'the Culture Secretary, Jeremy Hunt' in that order – never the reverse.

Stephanie Stevenson
St Martin, Guernsey

SIR – Could someone kindly explain why the BBC has suddenly stopped talking about *Bachkrain* and reverted to *Barrrain*? No wonder Britons are confused about their own national identity.

Emma Isworth
Tenterden, Kent

SIR – Is there not some central authority that resolves the correct way to render Arabic names into western script? Is it: Gadaffi, al-Gaddafi, al-

Qadhafi or Qadaffi; al-Qaida or al-Qaeda; Moussa Koussa or Musa Kusa?

The nation deserves to know.

Ken Stevens
Sonning Common, Oxfordshire

SIR — Most of the commentators on the death of Osama bin Laden pronounce the name of the town where he was killed as *Ab-BOT-abad*, with the stress on the second syllable, as if it were a local name.

But as I know well, having been stationed there for a couple of weeks in July 1944, the town was founded in the mid-nineteenth century by Major Abbott, an Englishman. It should be pronounced *AB-bot-abad*.

Guy de Moubray
Knodishall, Suffolk

SIR — I sympathise with complaints regarding the pronunciations of foreign place names in the news. I long for the day when the BBC and others cease pronouncing M-y-a-n-m-a-r as *Burma*.

Ronald James Button
Haywards Heath, West Sussex

SIR — *The Daily Telegraph* often publishes letters from concerned readers regarding their dislikes in today's grammar, but what good is it doing?

When I was at school, people who pronounced *th* as *f* or *v* were a rarity. Today it is unusual to hear anyone pronounce it correctly.

Will we soon find *th* replaced in the Oxford 'English' Dictionary? I hope I'm not around to see it. It seems that grammar is destined soon to be an item only on the Obituaries page.

Keith Kneebone
Camborne, Cornwall

THE MANCHESTER BROADCASTING CORPORATION

SIR – Following the BBC's move to Manchester, will newsreaders now change their pronunciation of words such as *bath* and *path*? As one of the majority of Englishmen living north of the Watford Gap, I often have great difficulty understanding newsreaders speaking in the manner of those living in the Home Counties with second homes in *Frarnce*.

BBC English has got to change if it is to be true to its new home.

Peter J. Newton
Chellaston, Derbyshire

SIR — Last Saturday one of those lookalike blondes who conduct fatuous television interviews with well-known former rugby internationals announced that England would shortly be playing *Franz*. I was left wondering whether we were to hear music by Franz Liszt or Franz Schubert.

Jeremy Wheeler
Byfield, Northamptonshire

LET ME BE ABSOLUTELY UNCLEAR

SIR — Has it become obligatory for interviewees on Radio 4 to begin their answers with the words, 'Yes, well, I mean . . .' and to include the phrase, 'Let me be absolutely clear', preferably more than once?

June Green
Lower Shiplake, Oxfordshire

SIR — Why is it that almost all interviewees begin their reply to the interviewer's questions by saying, 'So . . .'? Do we have media coaching companies to blame?

David Dixey
Stanway, Essex

SIR – Why is it that no one on the radio and the television can speak without saying 'in terms of'? Some people even say it after every sentence.

It is only with extreme self-control that I have managed not to carry out an act of violence against both media.

When did this nasty irritant start? Who started it? And why did everyone start using it?

I have managed to get by without using it once.

Julia Gallaway
Barnet, Hertfordshire

SIR – Am I alone in finding the ever-increasing use of the infantile word *scary* – particularly by broadcasters who should know better – rather frightening?

Richard Widenka
Battle, East Sussex

SIR – Why do the BBC and other broadcasters always seem to refer to children as baby goats? What am I supposed to do? Bleat in reply?

Julia Gibb (aged 14)
Leigh-on-Sea, Essex

SIR – 'I'm not doing too bad' was heard recently in a BBC broadcast. What is happening to the adverb? It seems to be disappearing from spoken English.

T. Bryant
Weaverham, Cheshire

SIR – When, oh when, are we to hear on the BBC the word *going* instead of *gonna*? I cannot remember it happening for the past year except by one 'educated' weather forecaster.

Margaret Lloyd
Sheffield

IT'S RAINING VERBOSITY

SIR – Am I alone in noticing the increasing use of expansive phrases when one word would do? Weather forecasters have started saying 'bits and pieces of rain', which I assume means showers, and 'clouds in the sky'. It is hard to imagine where else they might be.

Richard Pinion
Marsworth, Hertfordshire

SIR – Will someone please explain to me why *mist* has become *mistiness* in weather reports, and why *ground frost* is now *grass frost*?

Philip Hoare
Clophill, Bedfordshire

SIR – Has *heavy* now been expanded to cover all weather conditions? You report the effects of *heavy*, rather than *strong*, winds at Scarborough, while the weather forecasters now predict *heavy* fog where it used to be *thick*.

Yours, with a heavy heart,

Eric Horniblow
Bridport, Dorset

SIR – Why do the BBC weather presenters greet us with, 'Hello there', as if we were passing ships?

Anthony Messenger
Windsor, Berkshire

NICE KNOCKERS

SIR – Your article about the consternation caused to residents of Henlow, Bedfordshire, by Nice Baps, the name of their bakery, brings to mind my regular visits to the village of Knockin in North Wales. I wonder if your readers can guess what the village shop is called.

David Brown
Lavenham, Suffolk

SIR – While posting some letters on Sunday my heart leapt when I noticed that the letterbox said, 'Your Mail will be Collected NOW'. Then I realised that the plate stating the day was upside down.

Colin Trounce
Verwood, Dorset

SIR – I know that the NHS offers a comprehensive range of services, however I was still somewhat surprised to see in my local hospital a closed door inscribed: 'Baby Changing Here'.

Now if only they had offered that service when my kids were young and miserable . . .

Barrie Saunders
Bromyard, Herefordshire

SIR – Waiting areas in hospitals are not the most joyous of places. However, a recent visit with my wife to the Eye Clinic at Southend University Hospital was made fully worthwhile when I read the following notice: 'Please have your distance glasses ready for when you see the nurse'.

John Downer
Benfleet, Essex

HOLY BAD PUNS

SIR – You report that the policing costs for the Holy Father's visit could hit £1.5 million. But surely this is only a matter of money for old pope?

B.C.
Voutenay-sur-Cure, France

SIR – One hopes that Prince William's sense of humour can be contained during the exchange of marriage vows: 'I Will: You Catherine'.

R H-W
Nanstallon, Cornwall

SIR – Should Ed Balls and his wife both lose their seats, could it be said that they have been given the sac?

> **N S-T**
> Hundon, Suffolk

SIR – I read that the actress Lindsay Lohan is to be charged with battery. One would expect that she would be placed in a dry cell.

> **S.R.S.**
> Farnsfield, Nottinghamshire

SIR – In your blouse-busting obituary of Jane Russell, might it not be more accurate to observe that *The French Line* was originally filmed in 38D, rather than in boring old 3D?

> **J.A.**
> London SW18

SIR – Simon Cowell is missing a trick: Cheryl Cole might not be right for the American *X Factor* but she is perfect for the *Yi Factor*.

> **N.P.**
> Matlock, Derbyshire

SIR – I have just been looking out of the window at a delivery van that couldn't make it up the village hill due to the snow. It was towed by Lord Howard of Rising, who was passing in his Land Rover: does this mean he is Lord Towed of Towed Hall?

> **R.W.**
> Castle Rising, Norfolk

SIR – I find it confusing watching the tennis at Wimbledon because the players have similar names *ova* and *ova* again, and it is sometimes difficult to know *vitch* is *vitch*.

> **M.E.**
> Winchester, Hampshire

SIR – Was Blatter's unopposed re-appointment a Sepp too far?

> **R.P.**
> Cheam, Surrey

SIR – The FA should nominate Dennis Skinner for the Presidency. That way we would have an honorable man getting the Ballsover.

> **J.H.**
> Bramhall, Cheshire

SIR – I appreciate that Julian Assange has been 'occupied' during the past 48 hours of the Ashes, but why didn't we get advance notice of the Wicketleaks in Australia?

P.E.
Grewelthorpe, North Yorkshire

ANTI-SOCIAL
MEDIA

HACK-TASTIC!

SIR – While agreeing that hacking into other people's telephones is totally despicable and should be severely punished, my wife and I – a couple who can barely manage to text – have a certain admiration for those who have the ability to achieve such things.

John Ewington
Bletchingley, Surrey

SIR – How did the man in the corner shop have a pint of milk, a white loaf and six eggs ready on the counter when I walked in? Is my phone being hacked?

Godfrey Solomon
Sicklinghall, North Yorkshire

SIR – I wish News International would get someone to tap my phone calls. The information gleaned might not be of great public interest, but I should like to pay off my mortgage.

Jeremy Nicholas
Great Bardfield, Essex

SIR – Will the arch-chubster John Prescott bubble to the surface to try and scab a few more quid? I can imagine that trawling his phone records would simply reveal the pie orders.

A.K.
Blandford Forum, Dorset

WIKI CLIQUES

SIR – I've just been listening to Julian Assange's solicitor going through the rota of the usual champagne socialist, bleeding hearts supporting his client. I wonder if anyone could complete the list for me; I am afraid I fell asleep at Bill Nighy.

Roy S. Goodman
Ashford, Kent

SIR – I suspect that, had the editor-in-chief of Wikileaks been named Albert Jones, or something equally prosaic, none of this fuss would have occurred.

Richard Elsy
Carlisle

SIR – Of all the countries in the world to be extradited to, the top of my list would be Sweden.

Robert Stevenson
Cheltenham, Gloucestershire

SIR – Perhaps the biggest surprise in the Wikileaks saga is to find the words 'American' and 'Diplomat' in the same sentence.

Neville Landau
London SW19

SIR – I am sending this letter via carrier pigeon to ensure that it is not intercepted. Please do not publish, unless you can assure me that there are no moles on your staff.

David Franks
Lesbury, Northumberland

THE END OF THE WORLD

SIR – I'll miss the *News of the World*, the paper that once gave us the headline, 'Nudist Welfare Worker's Model Wife Falls For Chinese Hypnotist From Co-op Bacon Factory'.

Stephen O'Loughlin
Huddersfield, West Yorkshire

SIR — The *News of the World*'s style of reporting sums up everything that is wrong with this once great nation of ours. I thought we'd evolved from the cave.

Chris Mann
Sheffield

SIR — Now that the *News of the World* has joined the ranks of the *Eagle*, what shall I read for light entertainment?

Ian Lewis
Alciston, East Sussex

SIR — In the penultimate edition of the *News of the World*, did the resident astrologer predict its demise?

Dr Bob Turvey
Bristol

SIR — Would it be true to say that Ross Kemp's most dangerous mission to date was when he married Rebekah Brooks?

Peter Fox
Dublin

SIR – Do Rebekah Brooks and the Archbishop of Canterbury go to the same barber?

Edward Allhusen
Moretonhampstead, Devon

SIR – Has anyone noticed the uncanny resemblance of Rebekah Brooks to Paul Whitehouse wearing a Charles II wig?

E.C. Lyall
Ettington, Warwickshire

SIR – Isn't it true that those whom the gods wish to destroy, they first introduce to Rupert Murdoch?

Collin Rossini
Bradwell, Essex

DEL BOY AND RODNEY MURDOCH

SIR – My rule of thumb when trying to judge people's integrity is: would I buy a second-hand car from them? Upon looking at the Murdoch father-and-son duo on television today, the answer is an emphatic No.

John Harvey
Budleigh Salterton, Devon

SIR – Should one trust a man whose pocket-handkerchief is made from the same material as his shirt? I only ask because James Murdoch displayed this strange affectation in your photograph.

Simon Baumgartner
Hampton, Middlesex

SIR – If Rupert Murdoch does not get prosecuted for alleged phone hacking, then perhaps he could get prosecuted for not wearing a seat belt in your photo today.

Roy Landon
Burley, Hampshire

SIR – I got a very nasty shock when I saw Rupert Murdoch on television. Old and doddering were the first thoughts that sprang to mind, then I realised that he is younger than I am.

John Jenkins
Bolton, Lancashire

SIR – If Mr Murdoch can sidestep the issue by closing the *News of the World*, presumably we may do the same with the Metropolitan Police?

James Grazebrook
Crendell, Dorset

SIR – See what happens? We get rid of the two top policemen in the Met and two hours later, we are in danger of attack from custard pies and shaving foam. Thank goodness for Mrs Murdoch.

T.A. Rickerby
Scotforth, Lancashire

SIR – The cameras showed Rupert Murdoch full face – until the shaving-cream pie landed. Was he in charge of the cameras as well?

Dr John Doherty
Stratford-upon-Avon, Warwickshire

SIR – As the BBC now sees fit to play jingly-jangly guitar muzak between items on the Proms concerts, I ask myself: could it possibly get worse if our television were controlled by Rupert Murdoch?

David Mendus
Fetcham, Surrey

SIR – Rupert Murdoch's wife, Wendi Deng, has shown loyal support, not to mention a very forceful physical presence. Where in this whole saga is Mr Charlie Brooks?

John Holland
Dovercourt, Essex

SIR – I am intrigued to hear of the Christmas party attended by the Chipping Norton Set, including David Cameron, James Murdoch and Jeremy Clarkson. Imagine: the man who is Prime Minister; the man whose nod and a wink made him Prime Minister; and the man every petrol-head in the land wishes would be Prime Minister.

Oh, to have been a fly on the wall.

Huw Beynon
Llandeilo, Carmarthenshire

SIR – I live one mile from David Cameron's constituency home in Chipping Norton and wish it to be known that I have not had dinner with Mr Cameron, Rebekah Brooks or Matthew Freud. Reputations are so easily lost.

Trevor Taylor
Spelsbury, Oxfordshire

THE INJUNCTION AFTER THE NIGHT BEFORE

SIR – Is a superinjunction the morning-after pill for celebrities?

Edward Valletta
Bolnhurst, Bedfordshire

SIR – Will the new word for being outed on Twitter be *Twouted*?

Simon Walsh
Great Bardfield, Essex

SIR – I am thinking of taking out a superinjunction so that nobody knows I am not having an affair. Don't tell my wife.

John Scott
Shefford, Bedfordshire

SIR — My wife and I are deeply worried that we might inadvertently name one of these people who have taken out a superinjunction. It would greatly ease our fears if the courts could provide a list of the names that must not be named.

Tim Baker
Petersfield, Hampshire

SIR — In the world of the sexual merry-go-round, I just can't make up my mind who's the luckier girl. The anonymous partner of both Andrew Marr *and* Ed Miliband (gosh)? Or Nancy Dell'Olioliolio [sic], who's dated both Sven-Göran Eriksson *and* Sir Trevor Nunn (crikey)?

It's such a heady brew of talent, sexual charisma and good looks that it's just too close to call.

Matthew Walters
Twickenham, Middlesex

SIR — I feel Andrew Marr has other things to worry about; from the photograph accompanying your article, it appears he is unable to tie his own bow tie.

Simon Perks
Headcorn, Kent

SIR — I was amused to read on the front page of yesterday's *Telegraph* that the leading actor with a gagging order had paid a prostitute £195. Was he dissatisfied with the service, or did he negotiate a £5 discount for cash?

Howard Cohen
Bushey Heath, Hertfordshire

SIR — It is easy to forget that, only two years ago, people of the ilk of Sir Fred Goodwin and Dominique Strauss-Kahn — that is to say, bankers — were referred to collectively by a rhyming epithet. How wrong we were.

Ken Wortelhock
Orewa, New Zealand

SIR — A gagging order on Jeremy Clarkson? Now that would be good news.

Chris King
Woking, Surrey

SIR — If the politicians, television and sporting stars put half as much effort into their work as they do into philandering, the country might not be in its current state, it might be worth watching television occasionally and the national sports teams might win something.

David Costigan
Gosport, Hampshire

SAVING RYAN'S PRIVACY

SIR – As a sports fan it was with some disappointment, but no little surprise that I read of Ryan Giggs' affair. To paraphrase Robert Bolt: To sell one's soul for Miss World is one thing, but for Miss Wales . . .

Dr A. Dyson
Southwell, Nottinghamshire

SIR – Looking at Giggs, my only comment to the attractive girl involved is *gustibus non est disputandum*.

Brian Potter
Wroxham, Norfolk

SIR – Ryan Giggs? I thought it was all about Ronnie Biggs.

Professor Martyn Rady
Ramsgate, Kent

SIR – I don't know who he is, but I do know all about his sexual antics. Can someone tell me please, which team does he play for and is he any good?

David J. Hartshorn
Badby, Northamptonshire

SIR — Premiership football clubs should request their kit suppliers to provide all-weather chastity jockstraps, for which only the manager would have the keys.

A.B.
Hindhead, Surrey

SIR — Believe it or not, there are some of us who could not care less about the private lives of footballers, or their animated menagerie of affairs.

As for the wretched prattle known as 'Twitter', I think we now have a vacancy where our minds used to be. What witless drivel it all is!

Collin Rossini
Bradwell, Essex

SIR — 'Ryan Giggs "spent £30,000 on baldness treatment"' is the headline for the lead story of the *Telegraph*'s online news this morning.

I despair, I truly do.

Dom. Peter Palladas
The Wolds, Lincolnshire

GAMES OF
SEVERAL
HALVES

DAME MATA HURLEY

SIR – The actress Liz Hurley is not getting the credit she deserves. By keeping Shane Warne fully occupied and unavailable for the Australian team, special undercover agent Hurley is playing a vital role in helping England retain the Ashes.

Hopefully, there is still time for her inclusion in the New Year's Honours List.

Niall Sweeney
Oxted, Surrey

SIR – Am I correct in thinking that I am now the only person in Britain not to have received a gong?

Michael Heaton NoBE
Warminster, Wiltshire

SIR – A number of Ashes Tours ago, one of the Australian batsmen, with customary politeness, described the English bowling attack as 'pie throwers'. I wonder what description he might consider appropriate for an Australian attack which conceded 517-1 and 620-5?

Eric Poppitt
Axminster, Devon

SIR – Ever since my father (72) and I (44) returned after a 25-year hiatus to the village cricketing fold, England's international fortunes have soared. As I reminded my dad, 'All pyramids are built on strong foundations'.

Well, it's a theory at least.

Dr Jonty Denton
MCC (Medstead Cricket Club)
Medstead, Hampshire

SIR – May I ask what has happened to modest behaviour in victory? I always thought 'crowing' was the preserve of footballers.

Dick Powell
Burton Joyce, Nottinghamshire

GOD SAVE THE ENGLISH FOOTBALL TEAM

SIR – I have just watched the start of the Italy v England rugby match and could not help noticing the verve and enthusiasm with which both teams sang their national anthems. If only our footballers could be encouraged to do the same – even to open their mouths would be a start.

Perhaps it should be the first condition of

selection, with prowess on the field taking second place.

Eileen M. Hughes
Wimborne, Dorset

SIR – I now know why Wayne Rooney does not sing the national anthem. It begins with the letter G, and Wayne has never progressed beyond F.

David Hughes
Chedburgh, Suffolk

SIR – I don't know who scares me more when they're in full verbal flow – Wayne Rooney or Colonel Gaddafi.

Ivor Yeloff
Hethersett, Norfolk

SIR – How can the Football Association attempt to control Rooney's outbursts with any credibility when their very initials are an open invitation to obscenity?

Granville Davies
Crowborough, East Sussex

SIR – Who has Rooney offended so badly? I was most impressed at a recent Stoke City match by the home supporters' command of basic Anglo-Saxon and their rhythmic obscene chanting, far beyond Rooney's capabilities.

In the good-humoured crowd were many women and children, most of whom seemed to know the trademark chants.

Those sensitive sports writers need to get out more into the real world.

Commander Alan York (retd.)
Sheffield

FOOTBALL'S NOT COMING HOME

SIR – So, England is not to host the 2018 World Cup. Who cares? If I want to watch a bunch of overpaid foreigners in England kicking a kiddies' plastic ball about, I'll pay a fortune for a ticket to watch a Premier League match.

Stephen Gash
Carlisle

SIR — I can understand that David Beckham, who makes his living by kicking a bladder around a field, should spend time with the spivs of FIFA. However, I hope that we will never again see the heir to the throne and the Prime Minister being drawn into such an unseemly activity.

Professor C. Vyvyan Howard MB ChB PhD FRCPath
Coleraine, County Londonderry

SIR — Whose decision was it to involve the Prime Minister, the future king and David Beckham in the bid team? Did drink play a part?

M.S.
London W8

SIR — How sensible of FIFA to go with Russia, eliminating at a stroke any possible suggestion of corruption.

David Howse
Barton, Cambridgeshire

SIR — Is FIFA football's equivalent of the EU?

Mike Laugher
Windsor, Berkshire

SIR – In light of the weather in December, would it not now seem appropriate to abandon the ill-augured World Cup bid and make a bid for the next Winter Olympics instead?

J.R. Ball
Hale, Cheshire

OLYMPICS: SLOWER, FEWER, MORE EXPENSIVE

SIR – Not satisfied with exchanging online terrorist bomb blueprints for cupcake recipes, it appears that MI6 has also hacked into the Olympic ticketing website and replaced it with a shambolic, incomprehensible mess.

Anthony Lord
Thornton-Cleveleys, Lancashire

SIR – So the French did win the Olympics in the end. The British taxpayer foots the bill and they get the tickets.

Peter Amey
Hoveton, Norfolk

SIR – For the first time ever I keep checking my bank account hoping that money has been taken out.

Sara Dickinson
Tadworth, Surrey

SIR – I have just had £69 charged to my credit card account. Apparently I have been allocated a latte coffee and two hamburgers.

George Plume
Ipswich, Suffolk

SIR – Am I alone in not knowing anyone who has been successful?

Judith Sibson
Morden, Surrey

SIR – Is the rumour true that Sepp Blatter got all the Olympic tickets he applied for?

C.D. Macdonald
Hadlow, Kent

SIR –

JUST SO YOU KNOW.

Boris Johnson and others.

Have of course 'fiddled' the Olympic ticket 'ballot'

so as to 'favour' the BBC and 'celebs' and others.

PROBABLY using Russian KGB 'software'.

A MASSIVE Abuse Of Trust.

CAUSED.

By YOU failing to 'deal' with Booth and Blair.

'So ****** it!

I'LL "have a go" too!

Like 'Gordon Gecko'.

After all, it's a 'victimless crime'.

C****.

cc UK Records

B.O.S.S.

'MI5'

'C'

Interpol

M

SIR – I am just writing this email to say that I think the Olympics is a pile of s***.

Charlotte
Colchester University

SIR – Why all the fuss about Olympic tickets? The only ticket I am interested in will be one to a destination where there is no television or newspapers. I cannot think of anything more boring than watching people run round a track, swim down a pool, jump over a stick or throw a lump of lead (although Wimbledon does come close).

Colin Anderton
Baltonsborough, Somerset

STIMULATING TENNIS

SIR – Might it quieten Wimbledon's women if they knew that their on-court cacophony sounds more like porn stars simulating orgasm than sports stars stimulating their game?

Mike Starke
Chale Green, Isle of Wight

SIR – Is tucking into bananas at Wimbledon out of fashion? I hope so. After the average ladies' rally these days, the sight of the contestants holding, let alone eating, a banana would be a little unsettling.

Nicholas Neale
Sheffield

SIR – My wife says that if the crowd all howled along with the player, then it would soon stop. That, however, would probably be seen as unacceptable by the All England Club.

Nigel Pearce
Oxford

SIR – I would suggest that, in future matches, one lady should be allowed to shriek and the other should be forbidden. A toss of a coin at the start could decide the issue.

Robin Nonhebel
Swanage, Dorset

SIR – Ladies' grunts I can accept. Ladies in 'shorts', I cannot.

Piers Casimir-Mrowczynski
Gustard Wood, Hertfordshire

SIR – My husband contends that women tennis players who stuff the tennis balls in their knickers tend to lose their match. Are there any statistics to support this?

Caroline Rofer
High Peak, Derbyshire

SIR – Am I alone in thinking that, instead of doubles pairs touching hands after every point, it would be preferable if they saved their affection for the end of the set and then gave one big hug/kiss? I find the constant hand touching infuriating.

K.S. Hall
Dobcorss, West Yorkshire

BRAVE BEARD

SIR – If the few wispy patches of straggling hairs, bravely but almost vainly trying to push their way through the Murray visage at Wimbledon, are being referred to in some parts of the media as a beard, I'm glad he's Scottish/British rather than English. South of the border men grow real beards.

Ron Hill
Leominster, Herefordshire

SIR – Looking at Andy Murray's clenched fist and terrifying grimace, I now know why Hadrian built his wall.

Geoffrey Tuffs
London EC2

SIR – Those mutton chops make him look like a Victorian policeman with a grudge.

Nigel Blair
Willingdon, East Sussex

SIR – If you put the Gillette advert on the front page and Murray on the back page, it might persuade him to get nearer to a razor.

Gordon Hall
Sheffield

SIR – If his mum and the lovely Kim really wanted to support him they should drop a big hint by appearing in the players' box in slippers and curlers.

Malcolm Allen
Berkhamsted, Hertfordshire

SIR – If Andy Murray and Tim Henman had played each other in this year's semi-final, it would have been a remarkable result: they would both have lost.

Jeremy Bally
Thruxton, Hampshire

'INTRIGUING' GOLF

SIR — Watching the field of hacks and journeymen knocking their balls into the Sawgrass Lakes at the Players Championship, I reflected that if pro golf does not find a star soon it is in serious trouble.

It was intriguing — but only in the way that a ladies golf club Bronze Section is 'intriguing', where the local rule is that the last lady to lose all her golf balls is declared the winner.

Dr John Cameron
St Andrews, Fife

SIR — I was taught to play golf in Zimbabwe. My caddie told me to ignore any advice on my swing when teeing off, and just say 'Severiano' on the back swing and 'Ballesteros' as I hit the ball. It worked most of the time.

I no longer play golf; my husband plays enough for the two of us.

Janie Estcourt
Coln Engaine, Essex

SIR – Your correspondent writes that golf must be the only sport in which players do not kiss and hug each other. This is quite wrong. I have never witnessed it in chess or bridge. And how would it be achieved in polo?

Stewart Reuben
Twickenham, Middlesex

BA (HONS.), SUNGLASSES

SIR – On a grey afternoon on the Thames a number of the crew members in the University Boat Race felt that the wearing of sunglasses was necessary, while those not wearing them had them perched on top of their heads.

Even Sir Matthew Pinsent conducted his post-race interviews similarly attired. Is our university system failing us by producing people who don't know when to wear sunglasses?

Guy Mathison
Wetheral, Cumbria

BLUE-BLOODED BANK

SIR – As one of the owners of the Royal Bank of Scotland, I am proud to sponsor the Six Nations

Rugby Tournament, but can't we get rid of the enormous RBS logo in the middle of the pitch? Players should leave the field of play with their kit stained green, brown and perhaps a bit of red – but not blue.

Jeremy Nicholas
Great Bardfield, Essex

BRAWL ASCOT

SIR – A fight on Ladies' Day at Royal Ascot resulted in eight arrests. There were eight more on Tuesday; eleven on Wednesday; and 22 on Friday, including five for drug-related offences.

I think I'd feel safer going to watch Millwall.

Anna-Lisa Jones
Richmond, Surrey

SIR – I noted that one of the men in the fracas at Ascot was wearing brown shoes with a blue suit – no doubt someone who bought all his own furniture as well.

Michael Wingert
Penn Bottom, Buckinghamshire

SIR – Bryony Gordon writes that Ascot is 'one of the few places you can wear a tea set on your head and not look in the least bit peculiar'. I fear she deludes herself.

J.M. Bradley
Wellington, Shropshire

SIR– Yesterday you published a photograph of a woman at Ascot with what appeared to be some sort of terrible growth on her head. Would you please pass on my deepest commiserations?

Roger Marsh
Morecambe, Lancashire

SIR – With the Ascot season over and the raspberry season beginning, may I suggest that the ladies' headgear could serve a useful new life as bird scarers?

Heather Howell
Felpham, West Sussex

SIR – Now I've seen it all! A button-down collar with a morning suit – dreadful!

Malcolm Watson
Welford, Berkshire

SIR – Despite the, er, variables of the modern Royal Ascot Race Week, can we please standardise the pronunciation of the place for all – *Ascut*, and not *Ascottt*.

Nigel Kenyon
Bridgnorth, Shropshire

LORD'S VS LARSSON

SIR – Why do some people go to Test Matches? My wife and I were at Lord's for the second day of England v Sri Lanka on Saturday. What looked like three generations of a family were sitting in front of us in the Tavern Stand. One was reading the *Telegraph*, another a Stieg Larsson paperback, another *The Week*, another a book on a Kindle (an electronic device my grandchildren say I ought to have), and two teenagers were constantly bent over their mobiles, probably texting. They appeared to take no interest in the cricket, and they left two hours before the close of play.

I am 'Bewildered' (as opposed to 'Disgusted') of Tunbridge Wells.

Paul Maitland
Tunbridge Wells, Kent

SIR – I last went to a Test match over 20 years ago and intend to do so again this year. Do you think it would be possible to buy tickets for a seat nowhere near the Barmy Army?

David Keep
Forest, Guernsey

SIR – The Barmy Army deserve a collective medal for out-shouting, out-chanting and out-drinking opposition supporters, regardless of their own team's performances. They show the world that unique, eccentric British quality of humour and optimism in the face of defeat; like the Dunkirk spirit, it is beyond rational analysis.

Commander Alan York (retd.)
Sheffield

SIR – Ian Bell was reprieved after his run-out against India at Trent Bridge because the crowd booed. So now when you go to watch cricket, you can actually take part in the game. The umpires are just there to assess crowd reaction.

Richard Hodgkiss
Cheltenham, Gloucestershire

SIR – If England is to assume the mantle of the best cricket team in the world they should at least make the effort to look the part. Alastair Cook is seriously unkempt, while Bell, Trott and Anderson appear to be incapable of rising sufficiently early in the morning to have a shave.

J.R.G. Edwards
Birchington, Kent

OLYMPIC FLAMES

SIR – Your article on the five favourites to light the Olympic Flame missed the obvious contender. Surely the sight of Miss Pippa Middleton sprinting up the steps would gladden the hearts of at least half the population?

Chris Hodson
Bargates, Herefordshire

SIR – Given the media's obsession with 'celebrities', it will probably be a surgically enhanced female, the latest discard of a Premiership footballer, or the winner of one of the many pointless reality shows that fill the television.

Charles Nunn
Upton, Wirral

TELEVISION
AND RADIO

HAPPY CHRISTMAS, NIGEL

SIR — So, farewell then, Nigel Pargetter, murdered by Vanessa Whitburn, the editor of *The Archers*, for being male, white, happily married and wanting his children to go to private school. The BBC sees it as its duty to lecture us on what dolts we've been to vote out a Labour government, so poor Nigel was tainted with the leprosy of being posh, just like David Cameron.

Above all, he committed the ultimate crime in soap land; he had a happy Christmas.

Christopher Sandeman
East Hill, Devon

SIR — Has there ever been a greater misuse of technology than the provision on Radio 4 Extra of the dratted *Archers* a day early?

A.C.
Binfield, Berkshire

SIR — If Helen giving birth early and Nigel taking a tumble off the roof of his country pile — both of which have been blindingly obvious for days — are the best the BBC scriptwriters can come up with after 60 years of *The Archers*, I say, sack the lot of 'em.

I was looking forward to Helen dying and the surviving baby being black, with Tony and Pat having to adopt it; Elizabeth going over the parapet with Nigel, so Lily and Freddie were orphans with humungous death duties; and Harry discovering that Fallon is a ladyboy.

Robert Warner
Aston, Oxfordshire

RADIO HUMANITIES

SIR – In my world we classify the various radio stations thus:

Radio 1 – Left school without O- or A-levels

Radio 2 – Two or three O-levels, but wanted to start earning

Radio 3 – First-class degree in unusable subjects, such as Ancient French

Radio 4 – Good degree, usually the Humanities

Radio 5 – Four or five A-levels, including Media Studies

Talksport – O-level Carpentry

I hope this helps during the campaign to replace white, middle-class, middle-aged Radio 4 listeners with people under-30 from various ethnic backgrounds.

John Fowler
Harrow, Middlesex

SIR – I would like a radio station dedicated to the male, middle-aged, middle-class, solvent, tax paying, self-financed, and bloody annoyed.

Andrew Smith BA FCA
Epping, Essex

SIR – As I have just celebrated my 65th birthday may I ask the BBC to make Radio 1 more appealing to my generation?

Peter Watson
Dorchester, Dorset

SIR – Today I had a listen to Radio 4 to see what all the fuss is about. Some geezer called Melvyn Bragg woz banging on with some others about nerves in your body and all that. Boring! Just like being back at skool.

He didn't ask none of them what there favourite pop song woz or whether Cheryl Cole shood get a job on TV in America or anyfink like that. No wunder me and my mates never listen to it.

David Pearson
Reading, Berkshire

SIR – Why do Radio 3 presenters between 7 a.m. and 10 a.m. have such irritating mannerisms? We are invited to text them with trivia, seemingly for

their own gratification. Then they read out a reply
from Dave of Dover. Who cares? Then we are told
to read a particular article in a particular
newspaper, and not to miss a particular broadcast
event. And if we are very good, we can have the treat
of 'something I've brought in especially for you in
my rucksack'.

Leslie W. Cook
Richmond, Surrey

SIR – While widening the appeal of Radio 4 towards
a mythical new northern audience is obviously a
matter of some priority, I would suggest that of far
greater concern is the mysterious disappearance of
the BBC Television studios. Have they already been
packed up and moved to Salford? Interviews now all
seem to take place on the stairs.

David Dixon
Hastings, East Sussex

PAY, WATCH, SWITCH OFF

SIR – It would be interesting to see BBC3's viewing
figures for tonight's offerings of *Snog, Marry, Avoid* and
Hotter Than My Daughter, which features a heavily
tattooed 40-year-old grandmother.

When will the Government sort out the BBC and

stop them wasting taxpayers' money on these minority programmes?

I am sure millions of licence payers would rather see an hour or two of cricket highlights.

James Jan
Tunbridge Wells, Kent

SIR — People shouldn't complain about the BBC's failure to cover cricket on television. No fewer than four peak hours on Saturday afternoon were devoted to darts.

Garth Hill
Berkhamsted, Hertfordshire

SIR — To watch cricket on television requires buying a package of sport, most of which I have no interest in at all. I am so glad food retailers don't sell their wares in the same way as Sky. If they did, in order to buy a tin of baked beans for my toast, I would be forced simultaneously to buy four tins of processed peas, three of apricots and a red cabbage.

Andy Weedon
Kingstone, Herefordshire

GLASTOWATCH

SIR – Now that *Springwatch* on the BBC is ending shortly, may I suggest *Glastowatch* as a sequel. We could watch flocks of BBC executives earning multiples of the Prime Minister's salary flying in for a little R 'n' R. Hidden cameras in their luxury accommodation could observe their mating rituals and a swingometer could measure their carbon footprint.

Michael Evans
Buckhurst Hill, Essex

SIR – The apt juxtaposition of two headlines in your Monday's edition made me smile. 'Glastonbury: is this the best party on earth?' followed by, 'An infernally tiresome trip to Hell' – introducing an unrelated theatrical review.

Jim Buckingham
Nuneaton, Warwickshire

SIR – I'm more than willing to take up an executive role at the BBC for £400k per year. My salary will be self-financing through savings such as:
1. Only one newsreader onscreen at any one time.
2. Nicholas Witchell can do all his reporting about the Monarchy from the studio, thus saving travel costs. This will also apply to other reporters patronising us in this way.

3. Any drama that requires music to be played over the top of the dialogue would not be commissioned.

I await the inevitable job offer from Mark Thompson.

Alan K. Hollowood
Tattenhall, Cheshire

SIR – Not only is the BBC dumbing down its programmes, did your readers notice that in the excellent programme, *Wonders of the Universe*, Professor Brian Cox was given an inverted Union Flag to stick in his sandcastle at Kolmannskuppe while explaining the principle of Entropy?

Michael Allen
Sudbury, Suffolk

STRICTLY COME DEMEANING

SIR – If Ann Widdecombe was looking for 'fun' on her retirement, and is obviously happy to demean herself, wouldn't pantomime have met her requirement better than *Strictly Come Dancing*? She would have made a wonderful Widow Twankey, or perhaps the back-end of a horse.

M.M.
Bedford

SIR – Am I the only person to complain at the incessant noise generated by the studio audiences on televised musical shows such as *Strictly Come Dancing* and the programmes used by Andrew Lloyd Webber to find the leads for his West End shows?

There is a continuous chorus of screams from what appears to a regiment of teenage girls. At home the sound is similar to the noise made by soldiers' boots during the Trooping The Colour.

I have written to the BBC and ITV, and their response was that it provided 'atmosphere'. Should my wife and I also start screaming and clapping at home?

I have never been to a pop concert, but I believe at those functions audience participation is encouraged. Does this now happen at West End shows?

Ernest Boynes
Tarporley, Cheshire

SNOW PATROL

SIR – Can someone tell television presenters not to walk towards the camera while speaking? It never looks natural, and soon becomes annoying. The worst offender must be Dan Snow, closely followed by Neil Oliver. Do they get paid a mileage allowance?

D.A. Roberts
Manchester

SIR — Why is it that television programmes insist on telling us in the middle of a programme what is 'still to come'? It is utterly infuriating.

Mrs A. Buck
Swindon, Wiltshire

SIR — There is a widespread malaise whereby many programmes are ruined by 'clever clever' production gimmicks. Among the most hackneyed are cutting from scene to scene every couple of seconds, grainy slow motion shots (usually in black and white) to indicate an historical event, and literal background music.

On Sunday's *Coast* so desperate was the director's desire to match the music with every scene that a piece on Friesian cows was accompanied by Herman's Hermits' 'No Milk Today'.

Jim Whitton
Osmotherley, North Yorkshire

SIR — Music that drowns out dialogue is one thing, but even more irritating is that tribal drum banging over the *BBC News*' headlines.

Terry Lockhart
Wyatts Green, Essex

THE 10 O'CLOCK BANALITY

SIR – Am I alone in finding that the more banal the items reported on television news, the more pretentious the introductory graphics?

Granville Davies
Crowborough, East Sussex

SIR – I dread budgets, not for the content, but for Robert Peston's subsequent commentary. Am I alone?

J.A.
Gomshall, Surrey

SIR – As Robert Peston is to the BBC what John Bercow is to the House of Commons – a verbal embarrassment – couldn't both organisations get actors to speak their words?

Brian Christley
Abergele, Conwy

SIR – Why does the BBC think it is right to have a senior citizen such as John Simpson reporting on the front line in Libya? I served in HM Forces and even they would not expect a senior citizen to serve on the front line.

L.J. Clarke
Burraton, Cornwall

SIR – Surely the Japanese have got enough to put up with without the BBC sending Jim Naughtie there?

Jim Dale
Wirral

SIR – I wonder if anyone else has noticed that product placement seems already to have crept in to the BBC: some 90 per cent of their reporters from Japan's disaster areas are kitted out with distinctly logoed quilted jackets by the same manufacturer.

I can only hope that presenters end up using the same outfitter as George Alagiah, in preference to the Oxfam reject outfits worn by Andrew Marr.

Philip Webster
St Albans, Hertfordshire

LITERARY QUESTION TIME

SIR – The most irritating thing about *Question Time* is David Dimbleby's insistence on using *man* and *woman* instead of *lady* and *gentleman*. Such phrases as 'The woman in green in the front row . . . yes, you' give an impression of discourtesy.

Occasionally, Mr Dimbleby's unfortunate practice leads to unintended literary or cinematic references: *The Woman in White*, *The Man in Grey*.

John Rook
Enfield, Middlesex

SIR – I suppose one gets a bit out of touch down here in Somerset, but I was surprised to learn that *Question Time* even had an editor, let alone an 'executive editor'. I rather assumed that the panel turned up, the audience asked the questions and the panel answered them (or not). Then everyone went home. Is that not how it works?

Charles Heathcoat Amory
Maundown, Somerset

SIR – I have been delighted to see other readers echoing my sentiments on *Question Time*. At least I can say to my wife that it's not just me. I am also on the verge of giving it the bum's rush. Ten minutes seems about the limit, with too many regular panelists dished up to bore us into oblivion.

S.G.
Hexhamshire, Northumberland

MIDSOMER MADNESS

SIR – Following the complaints concerning ethnic diversity in *Midsomer Murders*, can we expect future re-makes of *The Railway Children* and *The Dam Busters* to contain a sprinkling of Somali refugees?

Lionel F. Goulder
Birmingham

SIR – Why does a firm the size of ITV jump like a scalded cat when these people open their mouths? As a veteran of the last war, I sometimes wonder why we bothered.

Derek E. Rose
Spofforth, North Yorkshire

THE EU-VISION SONG CONTEST

SIR – On Saturday my children made me endure an evening of excruciating auditory torment listening to the Eurovision Song Contest. Since then I have had an almost uncontrollable urge to join UKIP. Does anyone know if this is a normal response?

Dr Alan T. Evans
Newburgh, Fife

SIR – Well done, Kate and Will! The international interest in your wedding dragged us from the no-hopers' spot into the top half of the Eurovision Song Contest. But what can we do to avoid the slide back into ignominy next year? And do we really care?

Alan E. Quaife
Loughton, Essex

ABLE SEAWOMAN KITTY

SIR – Surely the biggest problem facing the producers of the forthcoming BBC adaptation of Arthur Ransome's *Swallows and Amazons* is not the story's disregard for health and safety, nor its possible lack of appeal to a generation brought up on computer games and blockbuster movies, but the name of one of the characters. Perhaps 'Kitty' would be a better option.

Anne Mills
Claygate, Surrey

THE ONLY WAY IS DOWNTON

SIR – Given that *The Only Way is Essex* – a reality television programme which follows the sad lives of a group of self-centred, uneducated, sex-obsessed, moronic young men and women from a county that has become a byword for banality — took the audience award for the best television show, beating the beautifully crafted and acted *Downton Abbey*, it is surely time to rename the Baftas the Daftas.

Robert Readman
Bournemouth, Dorset

SIR — Colin Firth's appeal was evident to British women a long time before he started winning awards. I was lucky enough to see him in the West End in 1983. I was so impressed by his performance that, for the first time, I waited at the stage door after the performance. He was a perfect gentleman and wonderfully approachable. I only wish now that I hadn't thought myself too cool to ask for his autograph.

Brenda Sherlock
Woodford Green, Essex

SIR — I thought I should go and watch *The King's Speech* to see what all the fuss was about. I must say that I have to agree with all the reviews that it was a splendid film, but I was a tad surprised that they chose an actor with such a bad stammer for the lead role.

Philip Williams
Forest Hill, Oxfordshire

HENRY VIII'S SIX ACCENTS

SIR – *The Tudors* has taught me so many new things about Henry VIII; I never realised he would occasionally affect a Welsh accent, or sometimes speak with a pronounced Irish accent. We're now just waiting for a Scottish accent.

Steve Long
Angmering, West Sussex

THE SUNNY ISLE

SIR – Am I alone in waking up in the middle of the night and wondering what the weather is doing in Ireland? The BBC weathermen and women studiously ignore the weather south of the border. Could it be they have better weather than the rest of us? And how does the weather get to Northern Ireland if it doesn't cross the south first?

I might just have to go to find out.

John Triffitt
Reighton, North Yorkshire

CORNERS OF
FOREIGN
FIELDS

THE DAILY BUNGA

SIR — Having just retired from work I am currently on holiday in South America. From time to time, I have sought to keep up with world news by checking your electronic website. Unfortunately, every time I do so a flashing warning — 'Adult Content' — appears and I am disconnected. In order that I may keep up with important world events, would you please arrange to stop printing the words 'Berlusconi' and 'Bunga Bunga'. Thank you.

Harry Royle
Colchester, Essex

SIR — Silvio Berlusconi's doctor is quoted as saying that the Italian premier may be 74 years old, but he is as robust as a 60-year-old and capable of having sexual intercourse up to five times a day.

I am 60 years old. Who's going to break this to my wife?

Graham Hoyle
Baildon, West Yorkshire

SIR — A question for your male readers: which would you rather be invited to — the Royal Wedding or one of Silvio Berlusconi's bunga bunga parties?

Stafford Trendall
Overton, Hampshire

SIR – Am I the only one who doesn't understand what 'bung bung' [sic] means?

Sandy Pratt
Lingfield, Surrey

SIR – Setting aside the morality issues, let's at least relish the opportunity Berlusconi's bunga bunga activities have provided *Telegraph* picture editors to adorn the newspaper with some cracking crumpet.

David Creffield
Lancing, West Sussex

PROTEST LIKE AN EGYPTIAN

SIR – I wonder if the anti-cuts protesters have learned anything from Tahrir Square and will in future clean up their nation's capital after their protests. I fear, though, that we may have to wait until our 'civilisation' is as old as Egypt's.

D.G. Dudley
St Asaph, Denbighshire

SIR – Given the peaceful overthrow of Hosni Mubarak in Egypt is Twitter more powerful than the sword?

Dr Colin Hughes
Midland, Western Australia

SIR – The last 12 months have proved disastrous for unelected, out of touch and unpopular heads of governments the world over. Hosni Mubarak of Egypt, Gordon Brown of the United Kingdom and Ben Ali of Tunisia have all been toppled.

Let us hope that Robert Mugabe, Mahmoud Ahmadinejad and Baroness Ashton are watching closely and sleeping less easily in their beds tonight.

Vere Bruce-Gardyne
London SW6

SIR – I see David Cameron's Big Society is proving most effective in the Middle East. Does this mean that he will now become an Internationalist like Tony Blair? Oh dear.

Robert C. Osborn
Bideford, Devon

SIR – Tony Blair invaded Iraq and Afghanistan, and now Cameron is invading Libya. Has someone been putting something funny in the water at 10 Downing Street?

John Ecklin
Great Bookham, Surrey

NO-FLIES ZONE

SIR – A no-fly zone over Libya seems an excellent idea. The Libyans have enough problems without flies.

Ray Cantrell
Colchester, Essex

SIR – Surely the most effective means of ensuring the no-fly zone in Libya would be to bribe their baggage handlers to strike; it seems to work every summer in Spain.

Anthony Lord
Thornton-Cleveleys, Lancashire

SIR – I presume that the British contribution to the action will consist of Messrs Cameron, Clegg and Fox standing off the coast of Libya in a pedalo throwing paper darts.

Neil Brook
Cambridge

SIR – Seriously, the Americans have a ship called *USS Ponce*?

Susan Ellis
Stockport

SIR – With regard to the report on today's front page of the possibility of the SAS seizing Libya's stock of mustard gas, am I correct in assuming this will be a surprise attack?

A.D. Dunster
Bournemouth

SIR – Following the SAS fiasco in Libya, isn't it heart-warming to know that Sid James, Flashman of the Fifth, Palmerston and Rudyard Kipling are still pulling the strings at the FCO?

Norman Davies
New Milton, Hampshire

SIR – The more footage I see of the to-ings and fro-ings across the Libyan desert of the raggle-taggle rebel 'army', the more I am reminded of the film *Mad Max*.

Let's withdraw the Nato forces – and just send in Mel Gibson.

Harry Hagan
Bury, Lancashire

SIR – Now that Syria seems to be attacking its populace, can I assume we will be intervening there as well? I reckon that the Tornados and Typhoons could, at a push, bomb Libya and route to Syria

through Akrotiri, Cyprus, and still make it back to
base for tea and medals.

Jerry Riley
Officers' Mess, Craigiehall, South Queensferry

SIR – It is reported that the Marks & Spencer in
Tripoli is still open and trading. Grantham's branch
closed at the beginning of the year. What does that
say about Grantham?

Steve Cattell
Hougham, Lincolnshire

SIR – Has anyone else noted from the newsreels how
pristine the Libyan road surfaces look compared to
our pothole-ridden roads? It makes you think
Gaddafi got one thing right.

Ronald Childs
Upminster, Essex

SIR – As Colonel Gaddafi declares an immediate
ceasefire in response to the no-fly zone, he once
more shows that he is not just a pretty face.

Tom Colborne-Malpas
London SW18

MUAMMAR'S MODESTY

SIR — Gazing in wonder and admiration at the beribboned chest of Colonel Gaddafi, it occurred to me: how come this gallant guy never made General?

James Young
Burnham Market, Norfolk

SIR — How come the spokesperson for nearly every Middle Eastern country is a 'Dr'? Most of them don't seem very bright. Surely they can't have all got their PhDs from the LSE?

Ian Thomas
Aspley Guise, Buckinghamshire

SIR — Where is Tony Blair when Colonel Gaddafi needs a handshake, a hug and a kiss? Is he in his counting house counting out his money?

David Hughes
Chedburgh, Suffolk

SIR — Am I alone in not having had my picture taken shaking hands with Gaddafi?

Viv Payne
Edwalton, Nottinghamshire

SIR – How long can Colonel Gaddafi last now? I am already monitoring eBay, hoping to get one of his wonderful uniforms for the Christmas panto.

> **Chris James**
> Llangernyw, Conwy

SIR – Is it true that Abdelbaset al-Megrahi, the Lockerbie bomber, is now applying for asylum in Scotland?

> **Julia Peters**
> Farnham, Surrey

FLASH-IN-THE-PAN GORDON

SIR – Surely allowing Gordon Brown to lead the IMF would be like allowing Colonel Gaddafi to lead Amnesty International?

> **Dudley E. Corson**
> Bradford

SIR – Following the furore over Dominique Strauss-Kahn, perhaps our Government will reconsider its opposition to the candidacy of our former Prime Minister to that role in the IMF. Notwithstanding the little matter of his trashing of the British economy, at least no one is likely to accuse Gordon Brown of being a 'hot rabbit'.

A.L.
Sherborne, Dorset

POWER SHOWER

SIR – Your correspondent expresses alarm at the increasing number of deodorants claiming 48-hour power. I too was perplexed by this until I saw one brand being advertised on television by Eric Cantona, a Frenchman; then it all made sense.

Liam Johnstone
Upminster, Essex

BIN LADEN'S DEATH SENTENCE

SIR – It is a pity Osama bin Laden was not taken alive. He could have been sentenced to go through airport security for the rest of his life.

Sandy Pratt
Lingfield, Surrey

SIR – Has Donald Trump seen the death certificate yet and given it the imprimatur?

Brian Stephens
Penarth, Glamorgan

SIR – The onus falls on al-Qaeda to post a YouTube clip of bin Laden playing donkey polo with a goat's head on a dust field in Afghanistan to prove he's alive – not on the US.

S.J.
Mid Glamorgan

SIR – I hope there will not be a spate of people trying to dance on Osama's grave.

Thomas Wood
Lastingham, North Yorkshire

SIR – It is scandalous that Sophie Raworth wore black while reading the news of bin Laden's death on *The Six O'Clock News*.

Prof Rennie McElroy
Penicuik, Midlothian

SIR – Clearly bin Laden made a fateful error in revealing his whereabouts in his 2011 census return.

Stephen Cheffy
Crawley, West Sussex

SIR – I understand that Michael Middleton, in his Royal Wedding reception speech, said words to the effect: 'When a helicopter lands in your garden, you know it's serious.' I wonder whether Osama bin Laden thought the same.

Dr R. Clipperton
Delamere, Cheshire

SIR – Maybe he took his own life after not being invited to the Royal Wedding?

Nicky Samengo-Turner
Hundon, Suffolk

SIR – Had the British been involved, I imagine we would have arranged for social workers to abseil into his compound and advise him to attend an anger management course.

John Bath
Worcester Park, Surrey

SIR – I don't want to be a party pooper about the Pakistanis, but they do cheat at cricket.

Les Nicks
Exeter

SIR – I suspect Lord Lucan is living in Camberley, a few hundred yards from Sandhurst Military Academy.

Duncan Rayner
Sunningdale, Berkshire

SIR – Judging by Hillary Clinton's expression, the Presidential party was actually watching Princess Beatrice's hat at the Royal Wedding.

David Richards
Surbiton, Surrey

SIR – What kind of a man chooses to attend an appointment to watch an assassination dressed in golf clothes?

Alan Green
Hurley, Berkshire

SIR – I am astonished that you do not seem, as far as I can see, to have published a word about the result of the Canadian election. Canada is a country dear to British hearts and your deep coverage of the death of bin Laden, which is ultimately less momentous, should not have allowed the election to be elbowed out.

Also, why do you not include Sheffield in your list of weather readings?

J.H.
London SW18

SIR — In all the millions of words about the death of bin Laden there has been no mention of the fate of the 40 virgins, poor dears.

Bill Dinning
Hornchurch, Essex

THE 'SPECIAL' RELATIONSHIP

SIR — With Barack Obama's visit to London in the headlines, there is much talk of the special relationship between Great Britain and America. Is this another example of the two nations being separated by a common language? Is *special* like *chips* — more substantial in British English than in American English?

Andrew C. Pierce
Bickington, Devon

SIR – The special relationship is sycophantic.
President Obama's unique speech to the joint
Houses of Parliament did not begin until 1548, 48
minutes late.

As a citizen of the US, as well as of the UK, I have
written to President Obama saying that he should be
punctual in future.

Dr Tony Hall
Harpenden, Hertfordshire

SIR – As a dog lover I find the description of Britain
as America's poodle more a term of endearment
than anything derogatory.

Edward Bryant
Paris

SIR – It was a shame that above your caption stating
that 'America has a large educated black middle
class', there was a picture of President Obama
holding his book upside down.

C.B.
Chilham, Kent

SIR – I note from their game of table tennis that our Prime Minister and the President of the United States of America are both left-handed; how sinister is that?

Graham Bond
North Weald, Essex

GREEK TRAGEDIES

SIR – Letting Greece join the euro and then being surprised when they're creative with their accounting is rather like inviting Errol Flynn to a house-party and subsequently being outraged because he got drunk and seduced your wife in the bushes.

John Andrews
Doncaster

SIR – Now the Greeks really have lost their marbles.

Lord Ironside
Boxted, Essex

SIR – Beware of Greeks spurning gifts.

R.M.
Ravenstone, Buckinghamshire

SIR – At Tesco today the cost for a tub of Greek Kalamata olives had risen from £3 to £4. We know the Greek economy is in a dreadful mess but how can a 33.3 per cent price hike in less than a week be justifiable?

Those are the last Greek olives I'll be buying.

Richard Dickson
Bridge of Cally, Perthshire

SIR – Surely the answer to the Greek crisis is to hold the Olympics in Greece every four years? It will also save the rest of the world an absolute fortune.

H.G.
Nether Compton, Dorset

SIR – If the Irish Euro cuts loose, will it be called the *Eiro*? And will the Greek be called the *Hello*?

Alastair Wilson QC
Tasburgh, Norfolk

SIR – The current problems within the Euro can be easily rectified. The four countries most in debt should leave the EU and form their own currency bloc. The banknotes could bear a trough with four large pigs feeding from it.

A.B. Bolt
Ash Vale, Surrey

SIR – Would it not be far less expensive and traumatic for Germany if she were to buy Greece rather than endlessly lend (if lend is the word) money? At one fell swoop the question of Teutonic towels on poolside furniture would be solved by a law that all should have the German Flag emblazoned on them.

John F. Collins
Groby, Leicestershire

WIR SIND ALLE BERLINE

SIR – According to *Der Spiegel* about half the British population is German. Certainly most people in my part of south-east England are related to Germans. They drive Beemers, Audis and Mercs and say, 'OK, yah.'

Ted Shorter
Tonbridge, Kent

TRAVELLING THE ROADS TO HELL

THE LONELINESS OF THE LONG-DISTANCE CYCLIST

SIR — As increasing fuel prices have forced me out of my car and onto my bicycle, I now 'enjoy' a 40-mile-a-day commute. There have been some very positive aspects to this: a two-stone drop in weight, £70 a week not spent on fuel and the smug satisfaction that comes from spending the savings on wine instead.

I've also been inspired to write a book: *S**t, Shoes and Road Kill — A view from the handlebars of Cornwall's cycle lanes and verges.*

Should anyone from the local tourist board wish to influence the title at all, may I suggest they ask the council to deploy the road sweepers a little more frequently?

No one likes cycling through a manky badger at 5.30 in the morning, and why is it always just one shoe?

Stuart Seear
Newlyn, Cornwall

NOT THE ORIENT EXPRESS

SIR — Recently I took my wife, who is French, on a trip to London by train. She was delighted. The wheels clattering over the points, the jerky swaying of the carriage, and the endless screeching stops and starts — all brought back childhood memories of the French trains in the 1960s.

Matt Minshall
King's Lynn, Norfolk

SIR — Celia Walden may find a young woman applying make-up on a train 'mesmerisingly awful'. She should count herself lucky. On a train out of Newcastle today I witnessed a woman applying under-arm roll-on deodorant.

Jacqueline Wells
Leyburn, North Yorkshire

SIR — Why on earth are the majority of seats on railway carriages upholstered in cloth? Judging by the carriages I travel on these seat coverings are hardly ever changed or cleaned. Meanwhile, the majority of Continental trains are fitted with a robust synthetic covering which is comfortable, easy to keep clean and surprisingly not too warm in the summer.

I know the British tend to encourage a healthy dose of dirt, dust and lice to protect our immune systems, but I would rather be the one to make that choice.

Michael Willis
Stirling

LESS HASTE, LESS SPEED

SIR – So high-speed trains will shave 20 minutes off the London/Birmingham journey. I am reminded of the man, who, brimming with pride, announced that he had shaved two minutes off his last car journey between Perth and Dundee. He was somewhat deflated by one of his friends asking, 'And what did you do with those two minutes?'

Iain Taylor
Kellas, Angus

SIR – It is pointless having a high-speed rail link to London when, on arrival, you have to queue for 20 minutes to buy a ticket on the Underground.

Mike Usherwood
York

SIR – Presumably Ambridge lies on the planned route and is to be demolished?

William Barter
Potcote, Northamptonshire

SIR – I've read all the shouting from the comfortable residents of Buckinghamshire with sadness and anger. I am longing for a high-speed train to Scotland. From London it is quicker to travel the 400 miles to Strasbourg than the 340 to Edinburgh.

I wish I did not have to grit my teeth for four and a half hours, trying not to use the awful lavatories and scanty buffets.

A.K.
Orpington, Kent

SIR — Last Tuesday I stopped at Reading services on the M4, as did a large number of men and boys, presumably coach parties going to or from some sporting event.

I have never before seen men having to form a long orderly queue for their lavatories. I could not help smiling as I thought to myself, 'There is a God.'

Mrs W.G. Chatham
Yate, Gloucestershire

PETROL PUMP HOKEY-COKEY

SIR — Whenever I refuel a hire car I invariably approach the petrol pumps from the side opposite to that of the fuel cap. I am used to this and shrug it off as just another example of the Law of Sod.

But now I know differently. Look at the fuel indicator on the dashboard and the icon of the petrol pump depicts the filling nozzle on the left or the right of the pump. This corresponds with the location of the fuel cap.

I hope this is a revelation from which your readers may benefit.

Philip Merivale
Keyhaven, Hampshire

SIR – Are there any petrol stations left in Britain where your car is filled up for you by a cheery attendant, who also wipes your windscreen?

Geoff Chessum
London EC2

SIR – I appreciate that I really should get out more, but I am intrigued to know why, after driving well over a million miles in 62 years (mainly in Britain), I have not once witnessed a Rolls-Royce parked next to a pump.

Alan Caville
Iteuil, France

ROAD HAGS

SIR – A new problem has arisen on small country lanes. Mothers from our local prep school have ditched their gym and Pilates – presumably due to the recession – and have taken up running after dropping the children off at school. They park their huge 4x4s and then jog along the narrow lanes in groups of three, accompanied by up to five free-running dogs.

If you try to pass them in a car or farm vehicle they shout and wave their arms at you in quite an aggressive manner.

Is there a new protocol needed here? Should one just follow at their pace or turn round and go home via a different route? Can someone advise, please?

David Corp
Doulting, Somerset

SIR – Am I alone in thinking that, in view of the myriad potholes on the roads at the moment, the police should now abandon the breathalyser and simply book any driver who is travelling in a straight line?

Louis Rayner
Plymouth, Devon

INDICATORS OF BAD DRIVING

SIR – I am hoping that some of your younger readers may be able to inform me of the new rules of driving. From my observations of drivers in Luton I have deduced the following:

1) Indicators are usually used to indicate a change of direction that you have already made.

2) In some circumstances indicators may be used to advise other road users of changes you are in the act of performing.

3) In no circumstances should indicators be used to advise road users of an impending action.

4) Motorists may pass through a red light so long as it's within five to ten seconds of the light having turned red.

Jeremy Bateman
Luton

SIR – I find that drivers who are likely to be a hazard to others – whether young, irresponsible tearaways or doddery old fools – can always be spotted well in advance. They invariably wear hats.

E.H.
Folkestone, Kent

MRS SATNAV

SIR – When I bought a Sat Nav (ours is called Gladys), I naively thought that it heralded the end to motorised, inter-spousal warfare. For a couple of weeks it worked: Gladys ruled and journeys were more relaxed.

Clearly unhappy about being replaced by a machine my wife came up with an ingenious solution. Under the guise of Health and Safety – Gladys would occasionally leap off the windscreen and distract the driver – Rachel now holds Gladys firmly on her lap, with the sound turned off, and gives me the instructions from the screen.

Everything is back to normal. Gladys is now firmly put in her place – as indeed am I.

M.S.

SIR – My husband spends more time reading the *Telegraph* and listening to the Sat Nav than to me.

Dorothy Baker
Edinburgh

SIR – I have a wife and a Sat Nav giving me directions when I'm driving, but if we ever get lost, somehow it's always my mistake.

G.B.
Smallhythe, Kent

SIR – If the expression 'jungle drums' is racially offensive, is it also racially offensive to have a TomTom in your car?

Nicholas Bielby
Bradford, West Yorkshire

FLIGHTMARES

SIR – I'm having a 'flightmare'. This is what you say when you are at the airport faced with cancellations for volcanic ash, strikes by baggage handlers or flight staff, bad weather, aircraft engine trouble, etc. It is a word which seems to be needed more and more of late.

Lindsay Bell
Isleworth, Middlesex

SIR – Now we know that the ash is made of larger particles than before, will they say the problems are due to 'the wrong kind of ash'?

Veronica Bliss
Compton, Hampshire

SIR – Why don't the Icelanders do something about their volcanoes?

David Hall
Banstead, Surrey

SIR — Yesterday, at Birmingham Airport, my friends had a garden hose spray gun confiscated in the security zone. When they asked what the problem was, they were told that 'the clue was in the last word — spray *gun*'.

Interestingly, it did not go into the bins where all the other confiscated items were put, but was placed on a shelf instead. I do hope the security guard manages to use it before the hosepipe ban comes into force.

Mary Channer
Bletchley, Shropshire

SIR — I listened to a banker on the BBC news this morning justifying the enormous bonuses they receive. 'If you don't pay big bonuses, you don't incentivise risk taking,' he told us.

Perhaps that's why I was never once paid a bonus during my career — I was an air traffic controller.

Gordon Bain
Ditchling, East Sussex

HORSE-DRAWN HAPPINESS

SIR — My wife and I have just returned from a very enjoyable weekend in Bath, where we took a ride in a two-horse cab around the city. We both remarked that without exception, wherever we went and whomever we passed, we were always rewarded with a smile. If only the aura of horse-drawn transport could be patented, the world would be a happier place.

Dr John Gladstone
Gerrards Cross, Buckinghamshire

DEAR *DAILY* *TELEGRAPH*

RANK PREJUDICE

SIR – There seems to be an increasing number of retired Service personnel contributing to your letters pages. My convention when doing so is to cite my former rank if it is relevant to the subject, hopefully adding some credibility to my view, but also revealing to the reader any bias or preconceptions.

On more general matters, I eschew rank. Might I commend this practice to others?

Capt. Brett Rayner RN (retd.)
Hailsham, East Sussex

SIR – I am continually surprised by those dreary old souls who persist in using distant military ranks.

Quondam F/Sgt. wartime heavies pilot Laurie Lloyd
Aldford, Cheshire

SIR – I see that on the letters page today, no fewer than five are signed by doctors. We soldiers, both serving and retired, had better get back to writing letters again before the quacks take over.

Lieutenant Colonel Richard King-Evans
Hambye, France

THE NORTH-SOUTH LETTERS DIVIDE

SIR – Over the years I have complained to successive editors about the extremely high percentage of letters from areas south of a line through Birmingham. I have on each occasion been blithely informed that you only receive a very small number of letters from north of Birmingham.

The situation is now bordering on the ludicrous; the line has moved south to just north of London.

The final insult as far as I was concerned was to be informed, for the second time in recent years, that a letter I had submitted had been included in a book of unpublished letters.

B.J.
Sheffield

SIR – I read the letters pages of all the quality newspapers. *The Daily Telegraph* publishes more letters from Lincolnshire than any of its rivals. How is this to be explained?

I.M.
Lincoln

SIR — Many years ago, when five pints cost £1, I drank in a pub in Eaton Terrace and was asked where I was going for the weekend. 'To Suffolk, to see my father,' I replied.

'Where the hell is Suffolk?' I was asked.

I explained it was one up from Essex on the coast.

Judging by the number of letters published from readers to this paper, and the house prices, London now lives here.

Patrick Wroe
Felixstowe, Suffolk

SIR — The letters page on March 31 contained three from Isle of Wight residents. That ought to quell rumours about our literacy levels.

Iain McKie
Totland Bay, Isle of Wight

SIR (or Madam?) — I see that in this Saturday's paper, you printed 18 letters to the editor. Sixteen of these were from men.

Lynda Clark
Kempston, Bedfordshire

SIR — I would be grateful if you could tell me when the best time is to submit a letter in order to maximise the chances of it being published. I don't have anything to write about at the moment but this would be most helpful for the future when something interesting comes to mind.

D.M.
Hitchin, Hertfordshire

SIR – I am an avid fan of the letters' pages. I have no witticism to offer immediately but would love the opportunity of some work experience in August.

N.A.
Manchester

Hi – I sent you an email a couple of hours ago by mistake. It was supposed to go to my wife, hence the love and kisses, which are something you probably don't get a lot of.

Apologies.

M.H.
Bocking, Essex

SIR – After many years of unsuccessfully trying to get a letter printed in *The Daily Telegraph*, or at least have one included in your books of unpublished letters, I have decided to move to Tonbridge and change my name to Ted Shorter.

Robert Holden
Westerham, Kent

THE TELEGRAPH FASHION POLICE

SIR – Will the Fashion Police at the *Telegraph* please stop going on about the Duchess of Cornwall, Samantha Cameron et al. 'recycling' their clothes. Dresses and hats are meant to be worn more than once, for goodness sake. Especially if they look nice and are well made.

Mrs S. Rose
Oakwood Bank, Northumberland

SIR – I'm thrifty; I've worn the same coat four days' running. I have also worn the same dress to every wedding for the last 20 years.

Shirley Copps
Cheltenham, Gloucestershire

SIR – The Duke of Cambridge appears to have worn the same suit on several occasions, though no journalist seems to know who designed it.

Graham F. Perryman
Higher Frome, Dorset

SIR – God forbid that Kate lends her sister a hat; it would be a world exclusive.

Graham Adams
Mitcham, Surrey

DEAR PICTURE EDITOR

SIR – Your report about Ofcom's ruling on 'Christina Aguilera's raunchy *X Factor* performance being on "the very margin of acceptable TV" was illustrated with a picture of young ladies holding their hands over their (clothed) breasts as if surprised while changing. Yet the report mentioned costumes that 'were revealing, with limited coverage of the buttocks, and were of a sexualised nature because they were based on lingerie such as basques, stockings and suspenders'.

Meanwhile, female backing dancers were seen 'opening their legs, kicking their legs up, gently thrusting their buttocks while bending over their chairs and leaning onto the chairs to position their buttocks towards the audience'.

Your readers are entitled to form their own opinions on this important issue, so please publish some more appropriate photographs.

Stephen Phillips
London SE24

SIR – Your report, 'Sun lovers enjoy warmest spring since 1659' was very interesting, but why show a photo of four women? Weren't there any men in Brighton?

Similarly, 'Greek Statues – a True Likeness' was also interesting, but why was there a photo of the historian but no picture of the ancient Greek statues? I'm sure many of your female readers will be as disappointed as I am.

Lynn Campbell
Weybridge, Surrey

SIR – What is it with your frustrated editors? Every weekend they appear determined to include as many photos of Nigella Lawson as possible. OK, she has creditable breasts but these are counter-balanced by an excessive posterior. For pity's sake, there are plenty of others with large chests, give them a chance!

Keith Haines
Belfast

SIR – Surely the point of Nigella Lawson's burkini was to create a cunning disguise. This way, she could avoid the perils of being bombarded by inquiries as to how much double cream to throw into one's cake mixture.

Stephen Jerrams
Stockport, Cheshire

SIR – The front-page photo on Monday, Tuesday
and Wednesday of this week have featured hats. Now
you have achieved a hat trick, could your male
readers possibly see something more interesting?

Eldon Sandys
Pyrford, Surrey

TOASTY, TASTY THOMPSON

SIR – Your columnist Harry Mount, a chap whose
views and judgment are normally pretty solid, has
fallen short of the mark today by observing that
Emma Thompson is 'not so hot anymore'.

I note in the photograph of Mr Mount, the fellow
is not wearing a pair of spectacles and is certainly not
anything other than a total struggle on the eye.

As for Ms Thompson, she was, is, and, judging by
the lavish way time is treating her, will remain for a
considerable number of years, toast and tasty.
Bonny, bonny woman!

If shown Botticelli's Venus, Mr Mount would no
doubt observe sniffily that she looks a bit too
Mediterranean.

Graeme W.I. Davidson
London EC1

WHAT'S THE STORY, MORNING FURY

SIR — What is Liam Gallagher doing in the *Telegraph* culture section?

Michael Rolfe
Rondebosch, Cape Town, South Africa

SIR — Can I get into trouble for saying that I have no wish to be inundated with media news, including a full page in *The Daily Telegraph* about Elton John's 'son'?

Tony Langford
Coventry

SIR — Am I alone in thinking that it would have been better for Elton John to have stuck to having a turkey for Christmas, like everyone else?

Colin Hunt
Weston-super-Mare, Somerset

SIR — As I sit down with my organic friends who cluster around my amazing success and popularity, may I vomit macerated dogs silently into my sick bag? Or maybe I'll go fishing and catch a pretentious egocentric carp. Please, *Daily Telegraph*, no more of this self-deluding bullocks about Trudie Styler's perfect weekend, or I'll never buy you again.

Ben Hopewell
Bath

SIR — The fact that the conical display of porcelain sunflower seeds at the Tate Modern was created by Ai Weiwei, a man whose civil rights are unjustly denied him, does not alter one iota the fact that the display is a totally unimaginative load of bollocks.

Keith Haines
Belfast

SIR — With every development in the horrible Bristol murder, we are updated with the current market value of everyone's house: victim, suspect and witnesses alike. Have I missed the relevance of this vital information? Have your crime reporters been moonlighting as estate agents? Or, in this time of recession, have your News and Property sections been merged?

L. Hamshaw
Frithville, Lincolnshire

SIR — Has the age profile of *Telegraph* readers changed while I haven't been looking? How many of us do you think can do Knee Crossover Tucks, Oblique Plank Raises, Single Leg Bridges and Single Leg

Bodylifts, as advised in your fascinating 'Get Fit For Summer' booklet?

Don't answer that. Just tell me instead: how many of the staff in the *Telegraph* office can do them?

Dr Jennifer Longhurst
Kingston upon Thames, Surrey

SIR – Am I now to conclude that *The Daily Telegraph* has gone the way of all flesh in its pursuit of modernity? One is grieved that this, the finest newspaper, has in recent months succumbed to the publication of scandal, but must we now also be subjected to the inferiority of modern Bible translations? For the first time, at least in my memory, the Text for the Day, from Hebrews 13.3, has been taken from a modern English version of the Bible (although one can hardly call it English).

Dr D.A.

INK FEVER

SIR – Am I the only person to have sneezing bouts as I peruse *The Daily Telegraph*? The ink has a distinctive smell and within minutes of opening the paper I begin to snuffle.

Brian Bloomfield
West Mersea, Essex

SIR – Am I alone in suffering frustration at the number of rogue vertical folds which appear on a regular basis in your newspaper and which detract from my enjoyment of what is otherwise an excellent publication? Unfortunately, unlike Her Majesty I have no one to iron my copy.

Graham Mountford
Aberdeen

SIR – For years I've head-butted the centre of the newspaper to fold it. I find I head-butt harder when I reach an article by Simon Heffer.

Peter Shirley
Chipping Norton, Oxfordshire

SIR – When I want to fold the paper my rather prominent proboscis works equally well.

Terence Edgar
Wallasey, Wirral

SIR – After completing the crossword on the back page, I use the 'knee-in-the-crease' method to fold to the Letters page. The smart crack this action generates serves to alert my other half that breakfast may now be served.

Michael Bacon
Farnham, Surrey

CROSS WORDS

SIR – This is the last straw. In a previous golden age I would turn to the back page and be able to fold my much-loved *Telegraph* into four. This morning I was aghast to see that the poor crossword had been moved to the depths of the paper, involving much judicious shuffling to gain access. This will prove a huge problem for crowded trains. I fully expect to have to iron the paper for my husband after I have finished with it.

Jane Hide
Malmesbury, Wiltshire

SIR – Why is it that as I get older, your crossword compilers conspire to make the clues more difficult?

Edward Hibbert
Hawksdown, Kent

SIR – Am I alone in finding it more difficult to complete the *Telegraph* crossword when it is not printed on the back page?

Chris Yates
Peasedown St John, Somerset

SIR – Am I alone in thinking the compiler of the anagrams is of, how shall I put it, mature years? Today's answers include *chaise longue*, *semolina* and *blancmange*. Can one still buy these?

Carol Thompson
Shepperton, Middlesex

SIR – The final frontier has been breached today. All manner of swear words can be tolerated in their context, but could one ever imagine that the dreaded *toilet* would be a solution to a crossword clue? This is a shock from which many of your loyal followers will never recover.

Simon de Boinville
Baughurst, Hampshire

R.I.P., SIMON HEFFER

SIR – What has happened to Simon Heffer? If he has left you, that is sad; if he has gone to another paper, that is bad; if you have told him 'you're fired', you're mad. Wednesdays, Saturdays and to a lesser extent Sundays are not the same.

Yet you still have the Tuesday lady's strange diatribes, unless in fact she is really a spoof. Is she a spoof? Then again, in years gone by I thought Sion Simon could not really exist as he wrote such errant

nonsense. Then he became an MP and I realised that
the unreal was real.

C.S. Holder
Bradford

SIR – Thank you for printing, so often and so
prominently, the words of the excellent Mary
Riddell, head cheerleader for the woeful Brown
administration. They never fail to remind me, when
my faith wavers, precisely why I voted Conservative in
May last year.

Robin Somes
Fawley, Hampshire

GORDON TONIC

SIR – Bryony Gordon expresses surprise at how
pleasant Jack Dee was when she interviewed him
recently. My wife thinks I am a grumpy old man. If
Bryony Gordon would care to interview me, I am
sure I could change my image.

Martyn Smith
Burnley, Lancashire

SIR – Further to my recent letter headed 'Bryony Garden', it should of course have read 'Bryony Gordon'. Sorry about that.

S.S.
Winterborne Stickland, Dorset

THE DAILY DEATH

SIR – So what is going to kill us off today? Bugs in the dishwasher, bugs in NHS pillows or an extra glass of wine with dinner? And for those who take statins they have the choice of a heart attack or diabetes.

How does anyone ever get to the end of the newspaper?

Les Sharp
Hersham, Surrey

A SPECIAL OBITUARY RELATIONSHIP

SIR – I usually enjoy reading about dead people and your obituaries page normally gives me the great pleasure of knowing I have outlasted them. What pleasure is there, however, in outliving three

Americans (Monday's issue)? Can't this country produce decent dead people of its own these days?

George Gaffin
Froncysyllte, Clwyd

SIR – Your recent obituary page was led by a homosexual cleric who became an expert grass-skirt dancer, followed by a virtually unknown American actress of little note. Meanwhile, an outstanding surgeon who pioneered maxillofacial surgery and an army captain decorated with the MC for outstanding leadership were consigned to the sidelines. While this might well reflect society's values just now, one would have thought *The Daily Telegraph* might have known better.

C. R. Champion
Banchory, Kincardineshire

SIR – In yesterday's edition of your normally excellent newspaper, the obituary to Osama bin Laden occupied a full-page spread. Why? 'He was evil, he is dead' would have been more than sufficient.

David Everard
Stockport

SIR – Among the many things I enjoy about the *Telegraph* is the sheer excellence of the research behind the superbly written obituaries. Every so often an endearing chink of fallibility comes along. Today the late Dr Chris Buckingham's most interesting obituary included the information that during World War Two he 'boarded a troopship at Galashiels'. Now that must have been quite a gangplank.

Roy McCallum
Glasgow

SIR – When I returned home from a cancer operation, your obituaries, strangely, cheered me up.

I used to spend many off-duty hours at Lord's as a member of the MCC, and at the Royal Albert Hall as a member of the Corps of Honorary Stewards. It was at the latter one evening that I found myself on duty at the top of the stalls.

Beforehand, as I stood beside a Loggia Box, three people advanced in my direction, heralded by flash cameras. One was Elizabeth Taylor, smiling and with an outstretched hand, which I duly kissed.

She held my gaze and to my astonishment said, 'My goodness, what beautiful eyes you have.'

I think I stammered something to the effect that, 'Well, yours are not too bad, you know.'

My word, from the neck up she was absolutely stunning.

Anthony Robinson
Exmouth, Devon

SIR — I saw your obituary of Prunella Stack, 'Britain's "Perfect Girl"', and wondered if she was as well-endowed as her name suggests.

John Hutton
East Molesey, Surrey

SIR — I have a giggle when I get to the Court and Social page. Those celebrating birthdays all have sensible first names, as do those who have died. But when I read the soppy names allocated by parents to their children, I can only presume they will have to shed their names when they grow up.

Bernard Sharps
Congresbury, Somerset

SETTING FIRE TO THE IPAD EDITION

SIR – How am I going to keep warm in the winter? You can't make paper logs out of an iPad.

Scott Clapworthy
Meole Brace, Shropshire

SIR – I, too, would be unable to cope with an iPad edition of the newspaper. Our *Daily Telegraph* has many uses: window cleaning; kitchen-bin lining and sheets placed in the hens' dropping pit.

Sometimes I even get around to reading it.

Roger Sykes
Earl Soham, Suffolk

SIR – Our guinea pigs wouldn't be able to use these iPad gizmos. We arrange the pages of the *Telegraph* to give them a mixture of news, and they then decide which part of the hutch is used for ablutions. Fred the Shred has attracted more deposits than anyone in recent times.

Jonathan Elderton
Cambridge

SIR – I wrap salmon in a wet copy of the *Telegraph*, then bake or barbecue it. When unwrapped, the skin of the fish comes off with the paper.

S.B.
Enford, Wiltshire

TELEGRAPH IS TELEGRAPH

SIR – I have to congratulate all those involved in the *Telegraph*'s Subscribers' Film Club. It is an excellent offer. However, after viewing *West is West*, which by the way was very enjoyable, I was rather saddened by the grossly overweight man eating crisps and talking through much of the showing.

This was compounded by the woman who strolled in 15 minutes late and then took five minutes to take off five layers of clothing before sitting down.

I find it hard to believe that these people are *Telegraph* readers, let alone subscribers. Please watch out for impostors.

Robin Bartlett
Hampton Wick, Surrey

FREE PETROL FOR EVERY READER

SIR — I notice that the 750ml bottle of water given away with the paper costs the same as the equivalent volume of unleaded petrol. Would you consider giving away the petrol instead?

Alan Taylor
Bury St Edmunds, Suffolk

SIR — May I thank Statoil for providing the paper-cover-advertisement on Friday's *Telegraph*? It doubled as an excellent barrier against the Scottish summer rain, keeping my copy dry and in perfect reading condition.

D.R.
Crieff, Perthshire

MAKING THE POLITICAL WEATHER

SIR — I am a Scot living in the Northwest Highlands. Although proud of my country I am also British and do not want the separation so strongly advocated by the SNP.

Alex Salmond and his cohorts take great delight in emphasising how careless journalism refers to England rather than Britain. An article you published yesterday talked about Britain having the hottest, driest spring since records began. My wife and I have just returned from two weeks of almost continual rain on the Isle of Arran. We drove here yesterday through gales, lashing rain and torrents of water exploding out of the mountains.

Please take more care and do not give further encouragement to the SNP's hot air.

Ian MacMillan
Wester, Rossshire

SIR – Can anyone tell me why the weather forecasts differ in national newspapers? Do they have different Met Office services, or do some newspapers just have a brighter outlook?

Derek Price
Worcester Park, Surrey

BORIS IS GOING DOWNHILL

SIR — Boris Johnson has once again been allowed to rant about ski helmets in your columns. Lovely chap, but has he got the safety interests of the skiing community at heart? I cannot help thinking that his stance has more to do with showing off his flowing locks than with issues of personal freedom.

E.S. Oldham
Winkfield, Berkshire

SIR — I am told that one of my ancestors had numerous children, all by different fathers. Interesting as this sounds, I am put off researching further by the knowledge that my mother's maiden name was Johnson. I don't think I could cope if it turned out that I am in some way related to Boris (and if he knew me, I'm sure the concern would be reciprocated).

Clive Pilley
Westcliff-on-Sea, Essex

PS

SIR – Sitting on a beach recently, the sun pouring over *The Daily Telegraph* while I buffed up the magnificent bazookas of a topless beauty nearby, I immediately grasped the madness of it all – hundreds of us laid out on a sandy curvature of the earth touching 1,000 miles an hour, a holiday humming-top of earthquakes, tsunamis, disasters and wars, soaking up the perilous rays of a gigantic nuclear furnace some 93 million miles away – and all the while eagerly awaiting the dulcet tones of a distant dinner gong to break the tedium.

> **Joseph G. Dawson**
> Withnell, Lancashire

SIR – Your correspondent asks if we have all gone mad. Mad? I am absolutely furious.

> **Martyn Pitt**
> Quedgeley, Gloucestershire

SIR – When I was a child in the 1940s everyone seemed to whistle. No one does these days. Why?

> **Mike Cole**
> Edington, Somerset

SIR – Following the end of the world yesterday, am I alone . . .?

> **Ian D. Spinks**
> Houghton Conquest, Bedfordshire

PPS

Dear Iain,

Of course you can use my letter. On the assumption that it will make the final edit, this will be a hat trick.

Curiously, I have had a more successful strike rate in *The Daily Telegraph* itself since your books started to appear and have even made the pages of the *Sunday Telegraph*. I doubt, though, if the two events are linked.

Best wishes,

Jeremy Nicholas
Great Bardfield, Essex

SIR – I have just received a very pleasant letter from your Iain Hollingshead asking if I mind you including one of my letters in your forthcoming book, *I Rest My Case*.

Of course I don't mind – but only one letter? All my letters have been the ultimate pearls of wisdom.

Dr R. Clipperton
Delamere, Cheshire

Dear Mr Hollingshead,

I am delighted and honoured to have one of my letters included in your book and shall certainly put it on my Christmas list.

Incidentally, I was recently filmed for a television series called *Narrow Escapes*. My programme, which is about the evacuation from Crete, should be transmitted about the end of October on the Yesterday channel.

It was my destroyer HMAS *Nizam*, which rescued Evelyn Waugh from the beaches. I count that as my greatest contribution to English literature.

Adrian Holloway
Minchinhampton, Gloucestershire